Praise for
101 Ways to Create
MINDFUL FORGIVENESS

Keep this book within easy reach.
It is a treasure trove of tips and ideas to help
you handle every hurtful situation.

The Reverend Canon Mpho Tutu van Furth,
artist, author, spiritual director

Writing a sensitive note is an art,
but choosing the right words requires some work.
In the pages of Kelly Browne's 101 Ways to Create
Mindful Forgiveness *are practical processes*
and guidance to help in choosing
those perfect words.

Robert Hickey, author, *Honor & Respect: The Official Guide to*
Names, Titles, and Forms of Address

Chapter by chapter, Kelly enriches our lives with
her internationally inspired tips and techniques for
mindful forgiveness right at our fingertips.

Pamela Eyring, president and owner of
The Protocol School of Washington®

T0026100

Author Kelly Browne solves the mystery on one of the most difficult topics: forgiveness. The is the new go-to book on how to forgive ourselves, release past pain and mindfully embrace peace to live your best life. Brilliant!

Elizabeth Hamilton-Guarino, founder of The Best Ever You Network and award-winning author of *The Change Guidebook*

101 Way to Create Mindful Forgiveness *is a book that will inspire all to pick up paper and pen to make a positive and powerful difference in this world. Kelly's suggestions fill the pages with words of acknowledgment, encouragement, and stimulate the heart.*

April McLean and **Debra Lassiter,** co-owners, The Etiquette and Leadership Institute and Perfectly Polished: The Etiquette School

101 Ways to Create

MINDFUL FORGIVENESS

Other books by Kelly Browne

101 Ways to Say Thank You:
Notes of Gratitude for All Occasions

101 Ways to Say Thank You! Kids & Teens

101 Ways to Say Thank You:
Notes of Gratitude for Every Occasion

101 Ways to Create

MINDFUL FORGIVENESS

A Heart-Healing Guide to Forgiveness, Apologies, and Mindful Tools for Peace

Kelly Browne

Bestselling author of *101 Ways to Say Thank You: Notes of Gratitude for Every Occasion*

Health Communications, Inc.
Boca Raton, Florida

Library of Congress Control Number: 2022948234

© 2023 Kelly Browne

ISBN-13: 978-07573-2458-1 (Paperback)
ISBN-10: 0-7573-2458-4 (Paperback)
ISBN-13: 978-07573-2459-8 (ePub)
ISBN-10: 0-7573-2459-2 (ePub)

Publisher: Health Communications, Inc.
       301 Crawford Blvd., Suite 200
       Boca Raton, FL 33432-1653

Cover, interior design and formatting by Larissa Hise Henoch

Dedication

For my parents,
Richard and Peggy Learman;
my children, Greta and Ava;
and my sister, Gretchen—who heroically
braved the journey at my side.

Contents

Chapter One
CREATING MINDFULNESS • 5

Chapter Two
APOLOGIES 101 • 17

Chapter Three
THE HEALING POWER OF FORGIVENESS • 35

Chapter Four
THE ART OF SELF-FORGIVENESS
AND SELF-CARE • 59

Chapter Seven

CHOOSING YOUR COMPANY OF FRIENDS • 113

Chapter Eight

STICKS, STONES, AND THE SCHOOLYARD · 127

Chapter Nine

WORKING DAY AND NIGHT · 145

Chapter Ten
ALL THE WORLD'S A STAGE • 163

Chapter Eleven
MAY THE FORCE BE WITH YOU … ALWAYS • 181

Acknowledgments

I want to thank every person who has crossed my life's path and become a light in the darkness when I lost my breath. I owe this book to my agent, Linda Konner, who is entirely responsible for its being. Thank you for *always* believing in me. My love to my mother, Peggy Learman, and Dorothea Johnson, who have been my greatest champions.

To the entire team at Health Communications, Inc., and Simon & Schuster, especially Christine Belleris, and the grace of my amazing editor, Darcie Abbene, who pushed me to go deeper, I owe you so much gratitude. Larissa Henoch, thank you so much for your beautiful design of the book!

Thank you to all the social workers and healthcare heroes at the Motion Picture & Television Fund and UCLA Health for your extraordinary love that became our compass. To the countless healthcare heroes at Children's Hospital Los Angeles: the trauma team, ICU Unit, and selfless nurses and doctors, especially Dr. Lindsey Andras and Dr. Lynn Osher at Valley Pediatrics, who saved my daughter's life. Thank you endlessly.

Rex Parris, Patricia Oliver, Dillon Sandidge, and Tom Phillips, as well as the entire team at the Parris Law Firm, your love and dedication on this Earth fighting for the greater good of humankind has saved lives for generations to come.

My dear friends who gave feedback and held me up: Kim and Warren Wileman, Carolina Bonino, LeeAnn Kreischer, Jan Galla, Dr. Shana Swimmer, Sue Kovacs Bellamy, Cindy Mays, and, of course, all my friends in the National Charity League, Inc., San Fernando Valley Chapter. Linda and my teachers at Hot 8 Yoga, who supported my healing journey, restoring my breath. My family, Aric, Jack, Mick, Edward, William, and Gretchen Learman Burrier, and the Mullens, Kerrigan, Gardner, and Fish families, my love always.

Greta and Ava, you are my entire life and my greatest gifts. I am so incredibly proud of the courageous women you are and love you endlessly. And to my father, Richard Learman, thank you for holding my hand on this painful journey. I love you and so appreciate your insightful and powerful writing, revisions, and comments that helped create this book. I could not have done it without you. I know Mom is so proud of us and the warriors we have become. Thank you for being my North Star . . . from the bottom of my heart. XO

Introduction

I have endured challenging situations as well as shattering life-and-death traumas throughout my life. We all have—it is part of our earthly journey. I am forever grateful to the countless angels that miraculously appeared when I tearfully prayed for help. Their divine intervention gave me the grace of strength when I could no longer stand. I share with you here the life lessons I have learned to help light your way so you may embrace this heart-healing path.

What spiritual sages say is true: The power of forgiveness and the ability to apologize are essential parts of our humanity. It applies to all of us, no matter who we are or what we do. It takes a lot of character to admit you are wrong, and even more to look a person in the eye and say, "I am sorry. Please forgive me." That single moment is a choice you make to either do the right thing or turn away.

Accepting an apology takes resolve. You are releasing that person from the negative energy bound to you over a hurtful incident. True forgiveness does not mean you are condoning or forgetting the difficult event that occurred, but that you are freely choosing to move forward in peace, enveloping yourself in love and compassion for your wellness. My mother would often observe, "It is better to be the victim than the one who committed the crime." I witnessed her moment of personal freedom from heartbreaking trauma when she accepted the peace she so desperately needed. Holding on to events that hurt us continues to cause us pain, dimming the light of our spirit and leaving us susceptible to illness.

In this heart-healing guide, you will be inspired by collected words of wisdom, sage advice, self-care, and reflective "Mindful Moments" journal check-ins to support you as you encounter conflict and search for insightful solutions for your wellness. My intention is to help you release the transformative, healing energy of compassion and mindful forgiveness—a positive force that may linger on to light the way for generations to come. The choice is yours.

With love + light,

Kelly XO

To err is human;
to forgive, divine.

Alexander Pope, English poet

The energy of the mind
is the essence of life.

Aristotle, Greek philosopher

Chapter One

CREATING MINDFULNESS

U pon our emotional earthly arrival, we cry, gasping for the *breath of life*, filling our lungs with air as we begin our extraordinary human voyage. In this pure moment of birth, it is instinctive that *our breath* is critical to our survival, for without it we would perish within moments. With our breath secure, we step forward into this new world encountering challenges and circumstances that will transform and shape us into the person we will become. We will pray for divine guidance and forgiveness, we will love and learn from one another, and experience the euphoria of happiness. During moments of pain, it is *our breath* that radically fluctuates when mindful breathing is essential to our well-being. As our physical body reacts, waves of discomforting emotion pass through us, and our thoughts race until we remember to pull back into the *present moment* and consciously begin to *breathe* again.

How do we get back to that blissful moment connected to our breath as people touch and break our hearts? How are we able to mindfully release what took us to our knees? By connecting back to our *breath*. Simply being conscious in this moment, clearing away all judgmental thoughts, and just *being*, that is the essence of being "mindful." Research has proven that when we are in that mindful state of being "present" and having an awareness of our *breath* connecting to the spirit of our life force, it opens the door to our power to *mindfully forgive*. By actively engaging in thoughtful meditation practice, we raise the quality, intention, and awareness of our ability to make amends. What you think, you become. In this chapter you will learn how to create mindfulness in your life.

The Basics of Mindfulness

We are conscious sentient beings with the ability to experience complex feelings. Going back to the essence of who we purely are, "mindfulness" is simply having an awareness, focusing our mind on being still without judgment while clearing out interior chatter and outside distractions. In this book you will discover "Mindful Moment" activities to help you cultivate mindfulness and open the path to forgiveness. To get started, here are a few foundational basics as we discover a mindful way of living.

What Is Meditation?

For thousands of years, meditation, in some form or fashion, has been a part of human healing, raising our vibration to a higher source. Simply defined, to *meditate* means to "think deeply or focus one's mind for a period of time, in silence or with the aid of chanting, for religious or spiritual purposes or as a method of relaxation." Our prayers are also a form of directed mediation, as are wishes and music therapy.

How to Meditate?

The human mind has different levels of consciousness and having an awareness of how we *feel* is crucial to our mental fitness. While there are different ways to meditate, the basic concept is to close your eyes and breathe slowly in and out, deeply filling your lungs. If you can shut out the world around you and focus on your breath for three minutes a day, it can shift your perspective on your life. When we can clear our minds and connect to our higher selves, it allows us the grace to consider our feelings and intentions. Embrace this moment, acknowledging the gift of your precious life.

The Spirit of Intention

Your intention is the *driving life force* that empowers the *idea* in your mind to manifest into the *goal* you desire to achieve. Being aware of your subconscious feelings is critical, especially when it comes to apologies and forgiveness, because our positive or negative intentions are actively directed toward what you want. Having that clarity of accessing your feelings when you speak to someone is important because your energy is transmitted with your words. If you have good intentions to create healing in a situation, that energy will be released to the recipient. The same is true for the bad vibes of ill intentions. The choice and decision of what you want to achieve are yours.

Meaningful Words for Mindful Intentions

Setting the spirit of your intention in your heart is important to creating the desired effect you want to release into the world. The following are some thoughtful affirmations to inspire you:

If my words or actions have caused harm to anyone in my life, I apologize and ask for the light and grace of forgiveness.

I release with love and light all negative thoughts and feelings about myself or anyone else, for the highest good of all.

I open my heart with love and gratitude for the blessing of my life.

I open myself to the healing grace of forgiveness.

I am beautiful, perfect, and resilient.

The divine light in me honors the divine light in you. *Namaste.*

What you think, you become.
What you feel, you attract.
What you imagine, you create.

Buddha, spiritual teacher

MINDFUL MOMENT: *Create a Vision Board*

Some of the world's most influential people manifest success by creating a vision board of what they want to bring into their lives. No matter where you are on your life's journey, you can create a vision of what you want to achieve and manifest it. Be it love, health, or career success, place an image of what you want on the board, directing your intentions toward those goals, communicating your desires to the universe. Take these proactive steps and believe that what you want is already on its way. Making a habit of setting a daily intention for yourself, like being grateful for everything you have, is a great way to start the day and create abundance in your life. Make the magic happen.

What is your personal daily "spirit of intention"?

_____

_____

_____

_____

What would you like to mindfully manifest in your life on your vision board?

_____

_____

_____

_____

What is it you plan to do
with your one wild and precious life?

Mary Oliver, American poet

Embracing *Shinrin-yoku,* the Japanese Art of "Forest Bathing"

Japanese research has proven that bathing in a forest atmosphere can reduce cortisol levels, also lowering the body's heart rate and blood pressure. By connecting to nature with our senses, forest bathing is not only restorative but also preventative medicine for our physical health. Making a habit of a simple walk while mindfully incorporating all our senses—sight, smell, sound, taste, and touch—can be transformative, allowing us to reconnect to ourselves. Creating this mindful space helps us to become more present and open to the benefits of forgiveness.

Here are a few sensory ways to enrich your forest bathing experience, wherever you are:

Sight

Silently observe all the details around you: the delicate beauty of the flowers, the texture of the tree bark, the vibrant colors that make up this very healing world. Notice how the trees release the dried leaves that no longer serve them.

Smell

Linger by the aromatic plants and relax as you deeply breathe in their fragrance. Notice the essence of the earth and the scent of the wet soil.

Sound

Close your eyes and listen to the sounds of nature, from the buzzing honeybees to hooting owls. Eavesdrop on the layers of living things.

Taste

Open your mouth and allow yourself to experience the taste of falling rain, wet snow, or edible plants. Many forest plants are used for their medicinal healing properties.

Touch

Feel the texture of the rocks, the silky wet grass, the brittle fallen branches . . . take it all in.

Forgiveness is a recognition that actions that are perceived as hurtful or wrong are the perspective of the small ego mind, not the higher self. The ego self feels the need to seek justice or revenge to right the perceived wrong. The higher self knows that the universe will rebalance all actions at the appropriate time and in the appropriate way in accord with the whole cosmos, not just the view of one person's hurt feelings. When you forgive, you are allowing that process to unfold, instead of holding on to your ego's point of view.

You are admitting that your limited mind doesn't know everything there is to know about what is right and wrong and you are recognizing that people's actions do not indicate what their true essence, conscious beings on the path to full awakening. In that sense they are just like you. Understanding that connection gives you compassion for them. From there it is a short step to forgive them and that reconnects you to your own spiritual truth.

Deepak Chopra, MD, Indian American author

THE SEVEN CHAKRAS:
Connecting Mind, Body, and Spirit

If you bend light through a crystal or witness a beautiful rainbow across the sky after rain, you experience the miracle of the brilliant colors of light that flow through the universe. In Hindu and Indian spiritual philosophy, the seven light chakras (wheels of energy) of the body create the core of spiritual power. That life energy *(prana)* radiates through the root chakra up to the head, connecting to the crown chakra. When one of these areas is congested with negative thoughts, feelings, trauma, and false self-beliefs, the light of that chakra is dimmed and clouds our mental health and connection to Spirit. Here you will find a brief guide to help you connect to your light chakras and their colors:

7 The Crown Chakra—Universe and Spiritual Wisdom

Located at the top of the head, the crown chakra is violet and represents a state of spiritual union, enlightenment, gratitude, and connection to the divine. A blocked crown chakra produces feelings of disconnection from a Higher Power, loneliness, attachment to material possessions, or fear of the unknown. Open up by embracing your *spirituality.*

6 The Third Eye Chakra—Intuition and Imagination

Located in the center of the forehead, between your eyebrows, the purple-colored sixth chakra is your third eye, representing intuition, perception, and imagination. Harnessing and developing its power, as you would exercise a muscle, are critical and allow you to be open to receive information, creativity, and ideas from the divine. When this area is clouded, it is difficult for you to see or sense situations with clarity. Open up by paying attention to *dreams* and *inner wisdom.*

5 The Throat Chakra—Voice, Expression, and Communication

Located in the center of your neck, the throat chakra is blue and represents the ability to speak your truth and communicate effectively. When the throat chakra is out of alignment, issues might include lacking the ability to express yourself confidently or not communicating your needs and desires. Open up by expressing yourself through *singing* and *speaking up.*

4 The Heart Chakra—Love, Relationships, and Forgiveness

Located in the center of your chest, the heart chakra is green and represents love and self-love. This chakra allows you to look at a situation from a higher perspective with love and to let forgiveness and healing come in. When this area is blocked, you may experience difficulties in relationships, depression, as well as a lack of self-discipline. Open up by expressing your *gratitude.*

3 The Solar Plexus Chakra—Power

Located just below your chest, the solar plexus chakra is yellow and represents your power, self-esteem, pleasure, and responsibility. When out of alignment, you may misuse power or exhibit controlling, manipulative behavior. Open up to owning your power by setting *boundaries.*

2 The Sacral Chakra—Creativity and Sexuality

Below the naval to the pubic bone, the sacral chakra is orange and represents your creativity and sexual energy. When this area is blocked, you may experience emotional isolation, sexual issues, and repressed creativity. Open up by mindfully noticing all the joyful details of life and experiencing *pleasure.*

1 The Root Chakra—Stability and Survival

Located at the base of the spine, the root chakra is red and represents stability and survival. This chakra connects your energy to the Earth by grounding. When balanced, you feel comfortable in your body; self-confident; and secure with friends, family, and your financial outlook. When out of balance, you might feel anxiety, fear, and isolation. Open up by grounding yourself and *celebrating* life with your family and friends.

It's possible not to know when you are out of balance. Releasing and moving blocked energy out of the body is vital for realignment on all levels. Spiritual healers embrace the concept that these dark areas of chakras must be illuminated to prevent sickness from entering.

Healing with Yoga

Whenever your chakras feel out of alignment, or you are simply feeling stressed, practicing the ancient art of yoga is an excellent way to restore your inner balance and promote healing. Participating in a group class, in person or via video, provides support and guidance. Or you can practice anywhere you feel comfortable. Simply move into the child's pose by kneeling, resting your belly on your thighs, and extending your arms forward over your head so that your forehead gently rests on the mat. Allow yourself to decompress and breathe.

MINDFUL MOMENT: *Embracing the Journey*

Every journey begins with a single step. What is the moment or person in your life you wish to mindfully release from your thoughts?

_____

_____

_____

_____

_____

How would your life be different if you could release the painful incident? Would you be happier? More successful in your relationships? Career?

_____

_____

_____

_____

_____

Have you hurt someone and wish to be forgiven? How does this desire affect your ability to extend forgiveness to others?

_____

_____

_____

_____

_____

What is one mindful action you can do today to support yourself as you walk the path of forgiveness?

_____

_____

_____

_____

_____

Feelings come and go
like clouds in a windy sky.
Conscious breathing
is my anchor.

Thich Nhat Hanh, Vietnamese monk and author

Forgive me, that I cannot sleep;
forgive the thirsty ones that have no water.
Forgive: if you never know forgiveness,
you'll never know the blessings that God gives.

Rumi, Persian poet

Chapter Two

APOLOGIES 101

The simple act of apologizing and taking responsibility for our words, actions, or choices that caused harm, confusion, or hurt feelings is a critical process across all areas of our lives. Expressed with the spirit of genuine sincerity, those three words—*I am sorry*—have the power to restore divided nations, heal the heart, or even save a life. Conversely, when a thoughtless word or act has caused endless pain and suffering for you or someone else, accepting an apology—*I forgive you*—is just as essential. Accepting an apology never erases the past nor changes the hurtful event, but it opens both parties to forgiveness, the possibility of restitution, and the healing ability to release those angry feelings so that you *both* may move forward in peace.

While it is true that the evolution of our ability to apologize and accept forgiveness increases as we mature from children to adults, having the mindfulness of our invisible connection to each other is essential, especially when we realize that the events that divided us might have been misunderstood moments to begin with. The wise recommendation "think before you speak" will always be true—words have the power to both destroy and heal. In this chapter you will learn the basics of how to apologize with sincerity and grace.

apology: *an admission of error or discourtesy accompanied by an expression of regret*

How to Apologize: The Six Rs

No matter how difficult it is to admit you are wrong and apologize, saying or writing "I am sorry" is critical to every relationship, whether personal or professional. The following are some basics to keep in mind regarding apologies:

Realization

You *know* you did something wrong. Unintentionally or purposefully, you said or did something that caused a person harm or led to hurt feelings.

Remorse

Feeling *sorry* or regretting what you did or said. If you aren't truly sorry, then the communication of your apology—the tone and inflection of your voice or written words—will not be genuine, and the recipient will pick up on this insincerity and perceive it as a false apology.

Reacting

Apologize as soon as possible for the mistake, even if it was an accident. Be mindful of your good intentions to reestablish peace in the situation. The spirit of your intention is key across every area of your life. If you say you are sorry because you feel forced, it will be perceived as a meaningless apology. Allow the other person the time and space to express their feelings when, or if, they choose to do so.

Responsibility

Take *action*. The sooner you take responsibility for the error, the easier it will be to repair and move forward.

Restitution

Make *amends*. Do what you can to make things right. If you caused physical damage, make it whole again to the best of your ability. Not only is it the right thing to do, but it will promote a faster resolution.

Resolution

After you have apologized, taken responsibility, and offered to correct the error, move on, and emotionally *release* the event. If the other person continues to hold the mistake over your head in the form of a grudge or refusing to forgive, you may choose to discontinue the relationship. Forgiveness is a process, and it takes time to heal.

MINDFUL MOMENT: *Creating Self-Awareness*

Take a step back and look at a difficult situation objectively. Can you recognize that your behavior, words, or actions might have caused harm to someone else? Or to yourself?

_____

_____

_____

_____

_____

Take a moment and try to see the situation from the other person's perspective. How might what you said or did have hurt their feelings, or possibly could have been misinterpreted or misconstrued?

_____

_____

_____

_____

_____

What was the spirit of your intention at the moment the incident occurred? What about as you move forward? How will you genuinely create healing and make amends?

_____

_____

_____

_____

What is the best possible outcome you hope to achieve?

_____

_____

_____

_____

_____

Dos & Don'ts of Apologizing

* Do apologize when you are wrong.
* Don't be a people pleaser. Never apologize just to appease someone.
* Don't beg to be forgiven. It is giving away your power.
* Do maintain eye contact so the other person knows you are sincere.
* Don't apologize if you don't mean it or if someone is forcing you to apologize.
* Don't over-apologize. You said it, now move on.
* Do be sincere in your choice of words and tone of voice.
* Don't agree when someone is insisting that you say you are sorry.
* Don't apologize for feeling a certain way or for who you are.
* Do allow the person you are apologizing to, to respond to what you are saying.

Sweet mercy is nobility's true badge

William Shakespeare, English playwright, *Titus Andronicus*

What's the Difference Between "Pardon Me" and "Excuse Me"?

The thread of forgiveness runs through our daily lives as we interact with others. When it comes to being courteous for interrupting or unintentionally causing a disruption, what is the best way to be polite when you want to apologize for the intrusion? According to Dorothea Johnson, etiquette expert, author, and founder of the Protocol School of Washington, Inc., "Using the phrase 'pardon me' in everyday social situations would be incorrect. Not only is it old-fashioned but a 'pardon' implies the request for forgiveness without a penalty. For what purpose are you asking for a pardon? 'Please, excuse me' or 'Excuse me' followed by 'Thank you' and 'You're welcome' would be most appropriate in these kinds of situations."

Taking Responsibility for Your Actions

It is important to take responsibility for your actions if you have caused harm to someone. It will also be far less painful to do so as soon as you realize the error. When you try to dismiss or cover up by lying, your dishonesty only adds more negative energy and will likely escalate the intensity of the situation, which might cause the injured person to retaliate or seek restitution. Remember, in today's world there is the possibility of not only a witness but also digital evidence of what transpired. Being dishonest or disingenuous will only compound an already difficult situation.

Three Faces of an Apology

An accident, incident, or hurtful situation can arise when you least expect it. It is how you *choose* to handle it that will affect the outcome. For example, imagine you are standing in line at the store. The person in front of you, distracted and not paying attention, steps on your toe. It probably hurts and you might impulsively react and say something. Consider these three possible reactions:

1. Immediate Responsibility

The person immediately turns around and apologizes in a sincere and meaningful way: "Oh, my goodness . . . excuse me." You might be in pain, but your negative reaction toward that person is likely going to be deflated because they immediately took responsibility. Now you can hopefully work with each other toward a resolution.

2. Complete Denial and Reverse Attack

The person who stepped on you glares wide-eyed and shouts, "I didn't step on your toe! You were in my way!" Now you might feel as if you must prove the injury. Maybe you think, *Yes, you did step on my toe, and now I am even more upset because you are making it my fault and shifting the blame!*

3. The Insincere Apology

The person looks at you, incredulous, and in an indifferent tone says, "Well, *if* I stepped on your toe, I'm sorry." You have a choice: Are you going to hold them to it and force them to admit their action? Or will you take care of yourself and walk away? You must determine how serious the offense is before you decide what kind of action to take or to simply walk away from it.

Whichever choice you make, take a deep breath before reacting in any way that could inflame the situation.

MINDFUL MOMENT: *Awareness of Our Reactions*

It's important to be aware and mindful of our reactions in any given situation that could arise. How would you react if someone accidentally stepped on your toe?

_____

_____

_____

_____

_____

_____

Reflect for a moment on how you might react if you stepped on someone's toe.

_____

_____

_____

_____

_____

_____

Without forgiveness life is
governed by . . . an endless cycle
of resentment and retaliation.

Roberto Assagioli, Italian psychiatrist

Respectfully Returning Property

If you took something that didn't belong to you, return it. Offering an apology and taking ownership of what you did is *always* the best course of action. Remember that when you take something that doesn't belong to you, there will always be negative energy attached to the item you took. Every time you look at what you stole, you remember what you did. If you no longer have possession of the item, buy a new one to replace it if you can. It is never too late to accept responsibility and correct a mistake. If you know you have committed a crime, consult an attorney and work with the proper authorities. Get it behind you so you can move forward in your life by restoring the energy, then you can release the act once and for all.

Electronic Apologies: The I'm-Sorry Text, Emojis, and Emailed Apologies

Communicating an apology when you believe (or know) you have hurt someone is important. The issue with electronic apologies for personal relationships and sending via text, emoji, email, or social media communication is that you cannot *see* the person's reaction. While you conveyed your apologetic sentiment, unless the recipient responds or has their "read receipts" on, you don't have verification that it was received or accepted. You also cannot read the emotion on their face or observe body language as you would if you were present. Unless they respond, you are left hanging. If you must apologize electronically, and it's a personal relationship, it might be better to make a phone call or video chat so you can hear each other's voices, see the person's face, and feel their spirit. What is important is that you make a sincere effort, with good intentions, to mindfully heal the situation with grace.

Meaningful Apologetic Words

The most important thing to remember in making an apology is to mean it and express it with sincerity. Here are some heart-healing words to support you:

I am sorry. Please forgive me.

From the bottom of my heart, I am so sorry.

Please accept my deepest apologies.

I apologize for hurting your feelings. It was not my intention to cause you harm.

I hope you will find it in your heart to forgive me.

This is long overdue. I am very sorry I hurt you during that time in our lives.

I understand now (that/how) my behavior caused you to feel uncomfortable.

I want to acknowledge that I deeply regret my actions that caused you or anyone else to be upset.

I apologize for my hurtful (words/actions/behavior).

I regret the choices I made. I hope in time you will be able to forgive me for my thoughtless actions.

I regrettably caused you pain and suffering, and for that I apologize.

I see now that I overreacted to the situation, and I am sorry for my unkind words.

I made a mistake, and I ask for your forgiveness.

To say that I am ashamed of my regretful behavior is an understatement.

There are simply not enough words to say how sorry I am and how I wish this never happened.

My (words/actions) were completely thoughtless. I want to extend my heartfelt apologies.

I should have considered the consequences of my reckless and insensitive (action/behavior) and how it affected (you/others).

I was rude and impolite. I apologize for my selfish behavior.

After the Apology ... Listen

Now that you have apologized, allow the recipient time to respond when they are ready to do so. They may continue to be upset despite your sincerity and not ready to just "get over it." Remember that anger is an intense emotion, as are hurt feelings, and when someone gets to that deeply anguished place, they need time to process and move it out of their body. It is also entirely possible that they may not be able to let their anger go, thereby ending the relationship with you. Rather than forcing, pushing, or begging a person to respond to you, give them the space to calm down. When they are ready to speak to you, keep these points in mind to help facilitate the needed mutual respect and compassion between you. Here you will find some strategies to help you navigate the moments following the apology:

* **I see you:** Look in their eyes, so they can see that you are listening, engaged, and open to hearing how they feel.

✴ **I want to understand:** Allow them to express themselves completely, without interruption. You may not agree with their responses; their words may upset you; or you may feel that they are overreacting. Be patient with them and with yourself. It is critical for them to express the anguish they experienced and for you to have the awareness of how your action affected them.

✴ **I hear you:** Just listen. Allow them to fully communicate their feelings. Don't roll your eyes or otherwise negate their experience of what occurred. Remember, it is *their* experience, from *their* perspective.

✴ **I feel you:** When they are finished speaking, reiterate back to them some of the key points they made so you are both clear on understanding each other's feelings.

✴ **I want you in my life:** You can each make a plan or present some thoughtful ideas on moving forward in an equally respectful way.

✴ **I release control:** One of the most important things to be mindful of in expressing an apology is understanding that you cannot control the other person's response after you have apologized. You can only express your sincerity and grace in your intentions to heal.

✴ **I need space:** If the recipient's response is mean-spirited, and they wish to continue to hold a grudge, or they can't move past the hurtful incident, it might be best to take a step back and review or release the relationship. Consider your health and welfare. Some relationships are not always meant to walk with us for a lifetime.

Keep in mind that everyone has a different set of life circumstances that color every reaction, response, and decision they make. Your words or behavior may unknowingly trigger an unfortunate event in their lives that has nothing to do with you. It is only when they can communicate something like "When you said _____, it made me think of how a person in my life had hurt me, and I felt _____." If they can be open, it allows the grace of compassion for you both. Some people also feel more comfortable staying in the "being mad" at you state. This behavior pulls the focus back to themselves in a needy way and could be controlling. This may be an addictive behavior, willfully creating drama, so others are compelled to walk on eggshells around them. If the cycle continues, you may want to reconsider your relationship dynamic with that person. Taking an active role in your healing is essential for your wellness.

It's one of the greatest gifts you can give
yourself, to forgive. Forgive everybody.

Maya Angelou, American poet

Unacceptable, Unapologetic Excuses

Every step we take, every communication we make—all our decisions are influenced by our experiences. These moments affect our reactions, how we apologize, and whether we choose the path of forgiveness or a route of revenge. Everyone is responsible for their actions. Manners, rules, codes of civility, and laws create boundaries for people with the hope of living together in a space of mutual respect and understanding. It is important to take into consideration how our actions, both positive and negative, affect others. When people make excuses for poor behavior, instead of taking responsibility, it can leave us feeling even worse. Always be mindful of the reality of certain excuses such as:

Excuse	Reality
I did that to you because you did it to me.	No excuse. Two wrongs don't make it right.
Oh, well, it's hard for that person to apologize.	Not an acceptable excuse for anyone.
Oh, well, that means they're sorry.	Really? How do you know their thoughts?
That person will never apologize; that's just how they are.	But is that acceptable?

Never ruin an apology with an excuse.

Benjamin Franklin, United States Founding Father

MINDFUL MOMENT: *Making Amends*

Take a moment to look back over your journey on this Earth and reflect on any difficult past moments you feel are unresolved.

If you could make amends with, or apologize to, anyone, who would it be?

_____

_____

_____

_____

_____

What would you say to them if you could speak openly and honestly?

_____

_____

_____

_____

_____

If you knew today would be your last day on this Earth, what step(s) would you take to tell that person how you feel? Would you call them, write them a note, or visit them?

_____

_____

_____

_____

_____

_____

Without holding anything back, what would you say?

_____

_____

_____

_____

_____

_____

_____

_____

_____

_____

_____

_____

_____

_____

_____

_____

_____

_____

_____

_____

When you apologize, you are restoring the dignity
that you have violated in the person you have hurt.
You are also acknowledging that the offense has happened.
You are taking responsibility for your part in causing harm.
When you apologize with humility and with true remorse
for hurting another, you open a space for healing.

Desmond Tutu and Mpho Tutu, authors, *The Book of Forgiving*

It takes a strong person
to say sorry, and an even
stronger person to forgive.

Unknown

Chapter Three

THE HEALING POWER OF FORGIVENESS

There is not a single person in the world who has not had a lapse in judgment, said the wrong thing, or behaved in a manner that caused someone harm. Intended or unintended, everyone will, unfortunately, not only inflict pain but also experience it. The decisions we make in handling these character-defining moments engage our ability to offer forgiveness and choose peace.

Harboring a continual negative stream of resentment, grudges, or hatred toward the person who caused you injury can make you physically sick. Studies have shown that holding on to those powerful painful feelings has a direct toxic impact on your wellness. Angry thoughts create stress in the body and, over time, can lead to illness and disease. As a dear friend pointed out, the word *disease* when broken apart is *dis-ease*. Such a simple observation can lead us to alter our mindset and embrace self-care. In this chapter we will discover the healing power of forgiveness.

What Forgiveness IS:

❋ Forgiveness is a daily choice you consciously make to support the release of your suffering. It takes time, patience, and self-love.

❋ Forgiveness helps you heal wounds and release toxic feelings from your heart, which make you feel unwell.

❋ Forgiveness is a choice that only *you* have the power to create in your heart and mind.

❋ Forgiveness allows you to take control over your thoughts and feelings, so you can release the emotional "mental time" that has kept you chained to a traumatic incident or a person.

What Forgiveness IS NOT:

❋ The act of forgiving does not condone the wrong that was committed, nor does it release the person who caused the pain from blame.

❋ Forgiveness is not a weakness, nor does it disregard the emotional impact of the incident that caused harm.

❋ Creating a mindful state of forgiveness does not mean that you are allowing someone to "push you around." Be self-assertive by having boundaries and standing up for yourself.

Mindful forgiveness is your mental decision
to consciously choose to disempower resentment
by energetically releasing the incident from your thoughts
rendering it powerless and moving toward inner peace
for your happiness and healing.

Moving Forward Toward Forgiveness

While many of us seek a quick-fix solution to our personal issues, when it comes to our feelings, they cannot be flipped off like a switch. Here are some thoughts to contemplate as you move forward toward forgiveness:

❋ It is not easy to get over a traumatic event that has hurt you deeply, especially when it involves loss of life, feelings, or the crossing of a personal boundary. It is a process that only *you* can choose for your healing.

❋ In choosing to release negative thoughts from your mind, you are not lessening the devastating impact of the event on your life, or accepting that the perpetrator is getting away with the offensive act. However, allowing toxic feelings to remain and fester in your mind and body creates the space for you to feel uneasy and depressed, which can create the space for disease.

❋ While you can never alter past events, you can choose to be empowered by taking control, and moving forward with your life so you don't stay stuck in suffering, feeling powerless. If a crime was committed, allow justice to prevail if it is possible.

❋ The event that happened to you in the past is likely not happening in the present, but the memory can be crippling, creating paralyzing panic and fear in real time.

❋ Forgiveness can only come in when *you* are ready to begin to release the events from your mind and body. No one can do it for you, and there is no specific timeline. It is deeply personal and sacred healing work.

❋ Consider when you or a loved one is facing a terminal illness or impending death. Knowing that you have limited time can create a spirited shift in your heart, allowing forgiveness to move in. Hurts you have been holding on to are now possibly outweighed by the desire to heal broken relationships. Will you choose to harbor resentment or create love and healing for yourself and those around you in this lifetime? Time really does heal all wounds.

Healing your heart is a process, which can be traumatic, especially if you are in a fragile state of mind, because it can cause you to "relive" the event. With the right self-care tools, you can equip yourself with the healthy information you need to begin to mend and bend crushed feelings into a more evolved, resilient, and empowered version of yourself.

The Forgiveness Thesaurus

amends	tolerance	discharge
pardon	purgation	compassion
absolution	clemency	amnesty
exoneration	mercy	acquittal
remission	pity	clearing
dispensation	lenience	pardoning
indulgence	quarter	vindicate
understanding	reprieve	releasing

Forgotten is forgiven.

F. Scott Fitzgerald, American author

Are You Holding a Grudge?

It is completely understandable why you might feel resentful when someone causes you harm and then refuses to apologize or denies responsibility. Not only does their failure to resolve the issue leave you hanging in shock and possibly holding your breath, but it adds a second layer of insult to injury. This impasse can make you angrier than the original incident. The reality is that holding a grudge, carrying resentment, or having bitterness toward someone or a situation over a past incident causes damage to your health. What self-care can you do when this complicated situation arises? If you feel you are carrying a chip on your shoulder, here are some ways to help you get clarity and support your wellness journey.

In Your Body

Holding a grudge is an intense negative energy that you create and direct toward the person with whom the conflict has remained unresolved. Even if the other person did apologize, were you able to fully release the injury and reconcile? Imagine creating a brick wall of resentment around yourself that is raised every time you see, hear, or think of the person who caused you harm. This is an intense, fierce energy that can quickly turn into hatred and last a lifetime. Think about what the energy of these thoughts is doing to you. The awareness of the harm you are causing to yourself is illuminating. Take the necessary action so you can shift it.

Turning Your Back

Are you refusing to speak to or respond to communication from the other person who is trying to connect with you? Are they aware of your bitterness toward them or why you are avoiding them?

Communicating your feelings is essential and has the power to resolve any issues or misunderstandings. You can look at both sides of a situation and decide if you want to continue the relationship. If you choose to end it because it is unhealthy for you, do so. Never worry about hurting someone's feelings if they have caused you verbal, mental, or physical abuse; your mental well-being and personal safety come first.

Pulling Focus

On the other side of this, are you or the other person being overly sensitive? Some people thrive on creating drama so the focus is constantly on them. They endlessly have issues and need constant care and attention. Known as *crazy-makers*, they can wreak havoc in your life. Pay attention to these patterns in yourself or others who always generate drama. This awareness can help you understand why you are creating the need for attention or set boundaries with someone who is demanding your time and energy.

The Stink Eye!

You know what this looks like! Even without words, the glaring eyes with raised eyebrows, a nasty scowl, or the silent shake of the head speaks volumes, sending a passive-aggressive message of bitterness. Think of the heavy energy you must expend from your body to communicate your anger.

Refusing the Grudge

If you ended a relationship because trust was violated beyond repair, the aftermath of that disconnection may hold consequences. Sometimes an offender can be incredibly manipulative and report to friends and family that *you* are the one holding the grudge, thereby shifting the blame as if they were the victim, perpetuating the drama.

Choose not to be on the defensive or report the facts of what happened. Take care of your own health and wellness. You can say, "I am leaving the past behind me and moving forward."

MINDFUL MOMENT: *Releasing Grudges*

Now that you have an understanding around what holding a grudge does to your physical body, reflect on the negative energy you create every time you see, hear, or think about the person or incident. Is your blood pressure rising? Is your heart pounding a little faster? Do you feel angry? How does it feel in your physical body?

_____

_____

_____

_____

_____

Remember, grudges are powerful toxic thoughts that are harmful when you continue to feed them negative energy. What choices and decisions will you make for your own self-care if the offender never apologizes? It's entirely possible that some people might not understand what you need from them. Will you continue to hold on to hatred and bitterness? Or will you choose to take the higher perspective that perhaps the issues from their past have nothing to do with you?

_____

_____

_____

_____

_____

Reflect on something that gives you great joy. How does this feel differently in your body?

_____

_____

_____

_____

_____

Compare the two feelings in your body. One causes excruciating pain or might trigger fear while the other might be euphoria. Remember, you are recalling memories from the past. What would you say to the person who caused you harm?

_____

_____

_____

_____

_____

Resentment is like drinking
poison and then hoping it
will kill your enemies.

Nelson Mandela, Nobel Peace Prize recipient

Self-Care Restitution: Take Care of *You*!

You are responsible for your self-care, so make your mental and physical health a top priority. Daily action to love yourself is the first step toward releasing suffering and allowing forgiveness to move in. For a shift to occur in your mind and body, you must commit to the work and be an active participant in the healing process to thrive. The following are some self-healing actions you can take:

Self-Love

If you don't *love* yourself first, it is difficult to make healthy choices that align with your best interest. Everyone is worthy of being loved, and no one has the right to make you feel unworthy without your consent! If someone is treating you poorly, reassess your relationship with this person or situation. Self-love is the greatest armor against fear and negativity. Love really does conquer all.

Self-Healing

If you are telling yourself that you will not be whole or well again, shift these toxic thoughts from your mind so you can begin the conscious release of the emotional pain you are holding.

Many spiritual healers will ask a person who is unwell what emotional trauma or false beliefs about themselves they are carrying. For example, perhaps someone once told you that you were worthless, unattractive, or would never amount to anything. While these are only words, they are very destructive, and without realizing it, you may believe these toxic thoughts. The emotional baggage you carry is caustic to the body and can cause physical pain. If the cycle continues, it will likely manifest in some form of illness in your body. Return those harmful words to the person who said them to you—they do not belong to you.

Breathe

If you've ever flown on a commercial airline, you've heard the flight attendants' instruction that should the cabin pressure fail, you are to put your oxygen mask on first, before rendering aid to others. Breathing is critical for survival. If you cannot breathe, or you are inhaling toxic fumes (or thoughts), what will happen? You will eventually be incapacitated and put yourself in a deadly situation. Be mindful of your breathing, especially when you are upset. Many of us stop breathing during a traumatic moment when the breath of life is essential to our survival.

MINDFUL MOMENT: *Feel Your Breath*

Lay your hand over your heart and close your eyes. Consciously take three to five deep breaths, releasing them slowly. Listen to the sound of the air coming into your body, filling your lungs. Be observant of the smells around you. Allow this simple ritual to become part of your daily routine. Do it when you wake up, in the shower, or anytime during the day. Take these moments for yourself. Breathe in deeply and slowly breathe out while visualizing the release of past negative situations, people, or incidents that are out of your control. Be present only in this moment. This daily practice will help you be mindful of your breath. There are also many meditation and breathing apps that will sync to your electronic devices, and hundreds of meditations are available on YouTube to support you.

Choose Compassion over Revenge

When a person has inflicted catastrophic harm against you or a loved one, the impulse can be to retaliate by taking some sort of revenge. Before you take any action, consider the following steps.

Choose Self-Compassion First

Step back and breathe, breathe, breathe. If you respond impulsively, taking the path of retribution, your emotional reaction may be worse than the original incident. Make a conscious choice to choose yourself.

Report the Offender

If a crime has been committed, report it immediately, and allow justice to take its course. When you take matters into your own hands outside the legal system, you may find yourself in just as much trouble as the person who committed the crime.

Let Karma Handle It!

If you believe in the concept of karma, that a person's deeds in this life will eventually come back to them in this life or the next, you can rest assured the powers of the universe know what happened and will seek to balance the harm.

Compassion for Your Offender

Try stepping outside a disturbing situation and looking at it from a higher perspective. What happened to the offender in their life that caused them to choose to cause harm to another? You may not care about their circumstances because this person's behavior was so egregious against you, but people can act out of anger because of their own personal pain and suffering. Why not make the cycle of anger end with you? Perhaps your conscious choice will be to deflect the negative energy vibes and recycle them back into the Earth, making a positive shift for good.

Put It in God's Hands

Whatever your spiritual beliefs, allowing God, a higher source, or Spirit to take control of the outcome of a situation creates the space for healing. Embracing the concept of releasing anger to a Higher Power to resolve is always in your best interest. My mother would caution me not to seek harm or retaliation against a person who had caused me harm, lovingly adding, "Vengeance is mine, said the Lord." I hold her biblical advice sacred to this day.

But I Am the Victim!

If you continue to hold on to what happened in the form of a grudge, you remain the victim because the offender's heavy energy remains connected to you. Yes, it is profoundly difficult to forgive someone for the act they committed against you but choosing to set a boundary by leaving the incident in the past is far more empowering.

Navigating False Accusations

Having the ability to rise up following false accusations against you takes tremendous moral resolve to handle the situation ethically. How do you find forgiveness when you have been falsely accused of something? Unfortunately, sociopathic people, with distorted thinking, exist in the world. Propelling themselves into the public eye, they personalize themselves as the victim, using catastrophizing words and misconstrued moments between you for financial gain. Internet trolls feed on the scandal, creating further salacious content for profit. Behind the scenes, someone's life is being ripped apart, affecting their families, friends, and careers. Before you participate in a public stoning of someone's character, consider if you have the ethical right to throw a stone in judgment at someone you don't know. What if this happened to you? Here are some thoughts to consider as you navigate this kind of situation.

Shock and Awe

Getting over the initial shock and awe of a false accusation is like a bomb exploding in your life. It catches your breath. Step back and breathe.

Gather Your Resources

If a crime has been committed against you, gather pertinent information and allow the authorities or your representatives to navigate the best course of action. Those who truly love you will stand with you.

Releasing Your Ego

Remember the spirit of your intention when you communicate by staying in the space of grace. If you are coming from an arrogant ego, your comments might be perceived as insincere.

Statement of Grace

Control your narrative with integrity and avoid going into seclusion, worrying about what people think. Not all false accusations garner a public statement, apology, or response, especially if the accuser is operating from a broken mindset. Depending on the circumstances, making a statement of grace and wishing for the best interests of that person can dissipate the situation. Not acknowledging false accusations is equally powerful.

Embracing Mental Fitness—Therapy

Nurturing your mental health is critical for self-care. Working your mind and thoughts out and talking about your feelings with a licensed therapist is always a good idea. It may take one session or many to get to the core of the hurt. In-person or virtual therapy allows you to tell your story in a confidential and judgment-free environment, so you can begin to release pain and begin the process of healing.

Ten Mindful Ways to Ground Yourself

When you are upset over something, you can put yourself into a state of fear and become "out of body," making it difficult to feel connected to your physical self. When we feel so detached, it is difficult to regain focus, so we go through the motions of the day without thinking.

Getting grounded restores your connection to the Earth by reestablishing your root chakra. Think of your feet on the ground like the roots of a tree, and mentally move back into your body. Be present in this moment so you can feel and experience the rhythm of your energy.

Holding on to anger is like grasping a hot coal
with the intent of throwing it at someone else;
you are the one who gets burned.

Buddha, spiritual teacher

Here are ten mindful ways to support your practice and honor your body:

1. Feel Mother Nature

Take off your shoes and walk on grass, snow, dirt, sand, or stone. Feel the texture between your toes. Lie down and look up at the sky, feeling the force of the universe around you. Allow the stillness to envelope you. Breathe, breathe, breathe.

2. Eat a Piece of Chocolate

Eating a piece of chocolate is an opportunity to practice mindful eating! Unwrap the chocolate slowly, feeling the silky texture in your hands. Smell the aroma. Break off a small piece and put it into your mouth. Allow it to melt for a moment, activating your salivary glands. Wrap your tongue around it as the flavor envelops your mouth. What kind of chocolate is it? Dark, semisweet, essence of orange, spicy? Experience the full explosion of taste in your mouth. Be in this moment.

3. Warm Salt Bath

The healing qualities of salt have been used for hundreds of years for detoxifying the body. Soaking in the rich minerals not only heals sore muscles but has a total-body relaxing effect. Infused with the calming properties of lavender or chamomile, it's a wonderful way to release stress. Envision the salt absorbing and removing the aches and pains from your body, washing them into the water, and down the drain, cleansing you of emotional baggage.

4. Ancient Yoga

With a five-thousand-year history in India, the spiritual philosophy of yoga is all about the discipline of breathing light into your body, clearing your chakras, and being mindful in the moment. Whether you attend an hour-long daily class in person or occasionally access one for five minutes online, practicing yoga is good for you, body and soul.

5. Mindful Meditation

Meditation is essentially the power of positive thinking, prayer, stillness, raising your vibration, and connecting to God, Spirit, or a greater force. Close your eyes and allow that enlightened energy to come to you. See the light, in all the colors of the rainbow, enveloping your body; visualize it moving all negative thoughts, beliefs, and heartache back into the Earth to be recycled.

6. Healing Tea

Enjoying a cup of good herbal, exotic black, dirty chai, or healing green tea—and allowing the complexities of the flavor to fill your mouth—can lift your spirits. Taking an afternoon tea break each day is a good opportunity to check in with yourself and see how you are doing.

7. Gratitude Journal

Every day write down three things you are grateful for. The more grateful you are for what you have in this world increases your positive attitude toward your life and keeps the gift of that positive energy flowing to you.

8. Sensual Aromatherapy

Aromatherapy can shift your mood instantly and provide a relaxing effect on the body. From lavender spray on your pillow at night, fragrant body creams, or a few drops of eucalyptus oil in your shower, scents have the ability to help bring you back into your body.

9. Earthly Nut Butters

Mindfully eating a spoonful of nut butter or a small package of raw nuts will help bring that satiating focus back to you. Known for their healing benefits, nuts and seeds, when incorporated into your daily diet, will improve your overall health.

10. The Magic of Crystals

The use of crystals for protection, cleansing your space, and alternative healing is an ancient practice. Choose a crystal that resonates with you, especially if it is to be worn as jewelry. Clear quartz, rose quartz, and amethyst are powerful crystals to clear and absorb negative energy, but others are magical too. Charge and recharge your crystal in the light of the sun and moon for twenty-four hours. Then bring it into the space you need to clear—your office or home or carry one with you in your car or bag.

Grounding is a conscious self-care ritual that deserves to become an integral part of your daily routine. Schedule it on your calendar, put it on your to-do list, or get up fifteen minutes earlier to make sure you take care of *yourself.*

Meaningful Forgiving Words

Energetically clearing the space between you and the other person is important. When someone finally says, "I'm sorry," avoid saying, "Oh, it's okay." Instead, accept it and say, "Thank you." Here are some healing thoughts and inspiration to help you find peace:

Thank you for the apology.

I forgive you.

I understand what happened. Let's move forward and put this behind us.

Please know that I forgive you, but every time I see or hear from you, it reminds me of what happened. For my self-care, I wish you the best. Maybe at some point I will change my mind, but for now I need to move on without you.

I am so appreciative to hear or receive your apology. I feel so much better.

I realize now that it was not your intention to cause me harm.

I felt deeply hurt by the words you used when you spoke about me in our conversation.

You no longer have control over me, my thoughts, or my feelings.

With love and light, I release you from all connection to me.

I understand you did not mean to harm me and that we are both coming from different perspectives. At this moment, however, I need the space for healing to take care of myself.

I wish you the best, but I need to let you go.

Let's put the past behind us and be more aware of our intentions when we speak to each other.

If you simply cannot verbalize how you feel but still want to repair a relationship with someone, a warm hug is a very powerful way to diffuse a negative space between people and begin the process of healing.

Embracing Emotional Support for Panic Attacks, Post-Traumatic Stress Disorder, and Suicide Prevention

The thoughts that race daily through your mind influence your choices and decisions. Crippling memories of an incident can suddenly explode to the forefront, bringing you to your knees. For many who have caused, witnessed, or suffered trauma, personal loss, or humiliation, the emotional side effects of mental anxiety can be excruciating. Creating the space for mindful forgiveness for yourself or for someone who caused you harm, or simply putting the past behind you, is important to our emotional healing. Paying attention to your breath, grounding, as well as reassuring yourself that the painful event is over will help, but it is vital to seek medical attention as soon as possible with a mental health therapist, doctor, or urgent-care facility if you are suffering from mental health symptoms. Remember, not all our wounds are visible.

Panic Attacks

The Mayo Clinic describes a panic attack as "a sudden episode of intense fear that triggers severe physical reactions when there is no real danger or apparent cause. Panic attacks can be very frightening. When panic attacks occur, you might think you're losing control, having a heart attack, or even dying." A smell, an image, a person, a name, a sound, or a place can be a trigger that catapults you back into a painful memory as if it were happening in the present moment. Symptoms may include fear of dying, suicidal thoughts, difficulty breathing, chest pains, the feeling of being in a tunnel, sweating, feeling overwhelmed, and depression. The gripping experience can last for seconds, or even several days.

Post-Traumatic Stress Disorder

If your anxiety is extended and interfering with your life in the form of vivid flashbacks, uncontrollable feelings, suicidal thoughts, or nightmares over a past event, you could have post-traumatic stress disorder (PTSD). While there are PTSD self-tests online, use them as a source to share your symptoms with your doctor to secure the appropriate medical treatment. For more information, visit the National Institute of Mental Health (www.nimh.nih.gov/health/find-help).

Suicide Prevention

If you don't believe in miracles, remember this: Life itself is a miracle. Your life matters, and you are on this Earth for a reason. Never let one moment or impulsive decision define you. My mother always said, "This too shall pass." It is really true. Keep breathing and focus on your breath. If your pain or anxiety spirals into feelings of self-harm, please get help immediately by seeking a mental health therapist, contacting 911 via text or call, or contacting the 988 Suicide & Crisis Lifeline via text at 988 or https://988lifeline.org/.

MINDFUL MOMENT:
Carrying the Stone—a Forgiveness Ritual

Taking inspiration from Desmond and Mpho Tutu's magnificent book, *The Book of Forgiving*, choose a stone of any size, shape, color, or texture . . . or let the stone choose you. Carry the stone with you in one hand, or fill your pockets with many stones, keeping them with you throughout the day. At the end of the day, set the stone in front of you. The stone is a symbolic representation of the burden of hurt you are carrying.

How did you feel about carrying the stone with you? Did it do anything for you? Did it help you to feel better? How?

_____

_____

_____

_____

How did you feel when you put the stone down and did not have to carry it anymore?

_____

_____

_____

_____

How do you think the stone felt?

_____

_____

_____

Did it feel like all your attention was on this stone instead of focusing on those people and things that needed your attention?

_____

_____

_____

_____

Did anyone know you were carrying the stone with you all day? Was it visible to others? Or invisible?

_____

_____

_____

_____

_____

How is carrying this stone similar to carrying anger or resentment?

_____

_____

_____

_____

Do you want to continue to carry the stone? Is it weighing you down? Or do you want to release it?

_____

_____

_____

_____

How would your life change if you released the painful incident or person from your thoughts?

_____

_____

_____

_____

Now that you have the awareness of how carrying this burden affects you, what steps can you take today to ground yourself, or what actions will you take for your self-care?

_____

_____

_____

_____

Taking a walk in nature, fragrant salt baths, a few minutes of mindful meditation, and simple deep breaths are good grounding rituals for immediate care.

We must develop and maintain the capacity to forgive. He who is devoid of the power to forgive is devoid of the power to love. There is some good in the worst of us and some evil in the best of us. When we discover this, we are less prone to hate our enemies.

Dr. Martin Luther King Jr., American activist

I've learned that I must find positive
outlets for anger, or it will destroy me . . .
I have to try to find a way to channel that anger
to the positive and the highest
positive is forgiveness.

Sidney Poitier, actor and author, *The Measure of a Man*

Chapter Four

THE ART OF SELF-FORGIVENESS AND SELF-CARE

One of the biggest challenges of the healing process is the uncertain space following a heartfelt apology. In that vulnerable moment, we hope to be forgiven as we solemnly promise to be more thoughtful in the future. We agonize whether the person will accept our appeal for forgiveness. Will they continue to be our friend, family, or lover and still include us in their life? Or will they choose to leave the relationship and continue without us? Will they say, "I love you; I forgive you?"

If you apologized with the heartfelt intention of healing the situation, along with your promise of restitution or the acknowledgment of your misjudgment, you must now release it and allow the other person to make the best choices and decision for themselves. Surrendering to the best interests of all involved can be difficult to accept, but it is the path of healing the energy between both of you. Someone else's decisions are not under your control. What is in your control are the actions you now create for your well-being.

The ability to forgive yourself and let go of the memories of hurting someone is vital in releasing your suffering, especially if the person chooses not to forgive you. If your prayer is to create harmony, so be it, and live in that grace. Continuing to carry self-hatred over something you foolishly did or said can be both physically and mentally destructive not only to you but also to those around you.

It is more difficult when a loved one refuses your apology and discontinues the relationship with you. What step would you take now? In this chapter you will learn about choosing the positive path of self-love, learning the lesson, and sage advice to get up and live again.

Self-Forgiveness: Recognizing "Unmindfulness"

The positive or negative thoughts you believe about yourself carry far more energetic weight in your subconscious than you realize. Every time you relive a moment of what *you believe* is a personal failure can instantly fill you with crippling feelings. If you think you will not succeed in life because you made the wrong choice, lacked motivation, or felt rejected with shame or humiliation, you have—perhaps unknowingly—accepted these false beliefs about yourself. In this debilitating state of "unmindfulness," you are holding destructive energy inside, consequences that can create anxiety and depression, leading to health issues. One way some people numb their emotional pain is by self-medicating with drugs, alcohol, food, or sex. While in that "intoxicated" state, they are *out of body* and often unaware of their actions and words, possibly causing irreparable harm to themselves and others. Essentially, they are surrendering the right to control their bodies to another force. When the effects fade, if they don't become mindful of their feelings, it can become a habit to reach for the drug that gave temporary escape—creating an addiction.

Addiction: Numbing the Pain of the Past

It is often a life-and-death decision to release the demons that surround addictions to achieve wellness. Some dependencies arise out of the need to disassociate the pain of a difficult past or current situation while other habits may be genetic influences. You may not realize you have an issue until it begins to interfere with your ability to function, overtakes your life, or becomes a dangerous situation for others. You can illuminate your pain by shining the light of awareness, recognizing what occurred, and getting the help you need to release it from your body. Only you have the power to shift to a healthy mindset to rebuild your life, which you can achieve by stepping toward recovery with support and self-care. Embracing sobriety and experiencing life, with all its joys, bumps, and bruises, takes dedication, self-love, patience, and self-forgiveness . . . one day at a time.

Forgiveness is not an
occasional act; it is a
constant attitude.

Dr. Martin Luther King Jr., American activist

Japanese Spirit of *Kintsugi:* Embracing Life Experience

Imagine a bowl is knocked to the ground and shattered into a million pieces—the epitome of how we might feel following a traumatizing incident. The Japanese spirit of *kintsugi*, "to be joined with gold," teaches that no matter what painful journey we have endured, we can put ourselves back together again into a more resilient and forgiving version of ourselves. By fusing the broken pieces of pottery with gold, like the fragments of our shattered selves, we make our imperfections more precious. Creating this mindful space for ourselves allows us to exchange the negative self-thoughts for positive self-talk and allow self-forgiveness to embrace us. Here are some mindful steps you can take to fill your veins with gold:

Embracing Yourself

Everyone's journey in this life is different. No one arrives on this Earth with a fairy godmother at their side. People may be born into families with more financial resources than you have, but it does not guarantee that they are happy or fulfilled. Life is what you make of it. Do you tell yourself that you would be a success if only you could go to a better school, or that if some horrible thing had not happened to you, or if only you had better opportunities? The perception of "success" is based on your thoughts and feelings. If you foster feelings of inadequacy—that you are not enough—that is what you will manifest to the world. Millions of people are happy simply because they are grateful for all their blessings. Taking an active role in your healing is a choice you make. It doesn't happen by accident. Aristotle's wise words, "We are what we repeatedly do. Excellence then, is not an act, but a habit" really ring true.

Embracing Self-Care

It is never too late to make a positive change in your life, no matter how small. A good place to begin self-care is by mindfully breathing, eating right, drinking water, and exercising.

Release the Drama

We can indeed get caught up in a dramatic situation, whether it is of our own or someone else's doing. Some people stay in that space because it is a familiar pattern. If you can take a step back and recognize your part in the cycle, it creates the space for healing. If, for example, you are creating full-blown emotional situations to draw attention to yourself—you refuse to let something go, or a loved one is doing that to you—it's time to step back and practice self-care mindfulness. Someone who consistently pulls the focus to themselves might be feeling that their needs are not being met. When you find yourself involved in something like this, stop and ask yourself, why do I feel this way? What is triggering my emotional response to this situation? What do I need to do for myself to feel better? Turn the attention back to you by turning inward and grounding yourself.

Return to Sender

If you've been told that you were stupid, unattractive, or that you would never amount to anything, these words reflect negatively on the mean-spirited person who said them, not you. No one has the right to belittle and intimidate you. These words can be a manipulation to coerce you to live according to others' expectations as an inadequate shadow of yourself. Take back your power. Return to sender! Give back these false words by visualizing those people sitting in front of you. Tell them that the false labels do not belong to you and that you are giving these words back to them. Then visualize cutting the cord of negative energy between you with golden scissors. Replace this energy with brilliant white light, surrounding yourself with love.

Embracing Change

If you are unhappy with your life but are not taking active steps toward doing anything about it, complaining about your circumstances will not provoke a change to occur. No one will change your life for you; only *you* have the power to do this. Start by making a list of what you want to change; then post it where you can see it every day. Do something every day toward your goal, no matter how small the step may be. You *can* change your life.

Embracing the Power of Positivity

There is something magical about the power of positive thinking. It changes your life by allowing you to accept your blessings with gratitude. When we shift our perspective, looking at a difficult situation with the spirit of our glass being half full instead of half empty, it moves us toward a positive mindset. Even when we experience excruciating circumstances, taking a moment to stop and reflect a positive attitude supports our healing. Stop and think about all the blessings in your life every day and watch them grow.

Hawaiian Prayer of Forgiveness

In ancient Hawaiian tradition, the spirit of the *Hoʻoponopono* prayer is to create healing in relationships between two people "to make them right again." Today, its intention has evolved to include love for yourself. Whether you choose to create the space to heal yourself or your relationship with another, the prayer's intention assists in clearing the energy of past pains and traumas. Hawaiian culture embraces the belief that withholding forgiveness may lead to disharmony in relationships and the opportunity for disease throughout the body.

Ho'oponopono, "To Make Right Again"

Please forgive me.
I'm so sorry. I love you.
Thank you.

First and foremost, we believe people can change. When we make a mistake, we need to admit it and then not run from it but stay and work to fix the mistake. And though no one can undo the past, we can balance the scales by doing good deeds and earning back our own self-respect, decency, and a legitimate place in mainstream society.

Dr. Mimi Silbert, Delancey Street Foundation

Ten Dos to Embrace Self-Forgiveness

1. Do remember to always love and care for yourself first.

2. Do get up every time you fall and try again until you get it right.

3. Do believe in yourself. Every day holds a new opportunity to manifest what you want.

4. Do allow yourself the grace to release the chains of another's harmful words or actions that berate or belittle you.

5. Do accept that you can achieve your personal goals; it is not too late to live your truth, to begin again, and to do it right. Time will pass anyway.

6. Do allow yourself to move forward and embrace life unafraid.

7. Do be mindful of what you believe about yourself and count your blessings.

8. Do create a list of what you want in this world and look at it every day when you wake up.

9. Do remember that you are a wonderful, magical person who deserves all the universe has to offer.

10. Do know that when you decide that you no longer want to feel disempowered by negative feelings, it will create the opportunity for healing.

MINDFUL MOMENT: *Self-Forgiveness*

We don't often stop and take a moment to ask *ourselves* how we are feeling. Remember, you are the expert in your domain, and only you have the power to access your thoughts. Simply checking in with yourself creates mindful awareness that will support your overall wellness.

Mentally scan your body. How are you feeling today?

_____

_____

_____

Is there anywhere you are feeling discomfort? Ask yourself what you need to do to shift that discomfort from your physical body.

_____

_____

_____

_____

What do you feel you need to forgive yourself for?

_____

_____

_____

How can you get to the heart of the matter with self-compassion so you can release any hurts you are carrying?

_____

_____

_____

Apologize to yourself. Go ahead . . .

_____

_____

_____

_____

What active steps are you taking to make amends for yourself so you can release the burdens you are carrying?

_____

_____

_____

_____

What daily self-care healing action are you taking to love and care for yourself?

_____

_____

_____

_____

Instead of mercilessly judging and criticizing yourself for various inadequacies or shortcomings, "self-compassion" means you are kind and understanding when confronted with personal failings—after all, who ever said you were supposed to be perfect?

Dr. Kristin Neff, cofounder, Center for Mindful Self-Compassion

Meaningful Self-Forgiving Words

When you are searching for a little self-forgiving inspiration to lift you up, use these words to empower and love yourself.

I acknowledge that I have learned a lesson from which I will grow.

I can be a light for others.

I love myself, first, last, and always.

I am worthy of love and happiness.

I am resilient, strong, and powerful.

I will use my voice and share my story to help others.

I will not allow one painful moment in my life to destroy what I have yet to live.

I have one amazing life to live; bring it on!

I embrace the beauty and magic of everything that I am.

I am so grateful for the adventure of my life that is still ahead.

Now I have the clarity to learn from this difficult experience so that I can grow from it, protect myself, and listen to my intuition or help someone else.

Who Do You Blame in Your Life?

Some people can engage in shifting the blame of responsibility away from themselves for their inability to reach goals; others rise in the face of adversity. No matter the set of circumstances you were given in this life, it's what you *do* that makes the difference. Many people have dire situations, but they grow and learn from their difficulties, using them to become better than their past selves. Take your life back and embrace it.

I got to a point in my life where I realized that I had to take responsibility for the decisions I was making as an adult and stop blaming my mother for what I felt she didn't give me. Using what I didn't get in my past as an excuse, blaming her for what was happening now—was no longer working for me. I had to claim responsibility for my life, nurture myself and truly own it. I wrote her a letter thanking her for all the things she was able to give me—having that acknowledgement of grace and gratitude allowed me to shift and move forward.

LeeAnn Kreischer, writer and podcast host of *Wife of the Party*

MINDFUL MOMENT: *Creating Self-Awareness*

Are you are making statements or excuses such as "If this had not happened in my life . . .," or "If my parent loved me . . .," or "If my boss believed in me . . .," or "If my partner would only . . . then I would have been able to . . .?" What excuse is stopping you from moving forward?

_____

_____

_____

_____

When you don't achieve your life goals, whom or what do you blame?

_____

_____

_____

_____

Who do you feel stands in your way, or hurts your self-esteem?

_____

_____

_____

_____

To begin healing yourself, what would you say to that person now?

_____

_____

_____

_____

Who encouraged you to believe in yourself and reach for your goals? If they have passed away, what advice would they give you when you needed it the most?

_____

_____

_____

_____

If you are unhappy with your life, what steps are you taking to change it?

_____

_____

_____

_____

Releasing the Stone—Recycling Negative Energy Back to the Earth

This is a powerful exercise for the physical release of anger and negative energy from your body back into the universe to create forgiveness for yourself, a situation, or someone else. The results are freeing and might create an unexpected emotional response. While the person is not physically present, or the event is not happening, you can call back that memory. Work within your own spiritual practice for support and create healing for yourself.

* Write your pain, or the name of the person you want to release, on the surface of the stone, or many stones, if necessary.
* Visualize moving the heaviness of that negative energy connected to those crippling memories from your body into the stone.

✱ When you are ready, release the stone back into nature by throwing it into a canyon, leaving it in a park, or skipping it into a body of water, and physically letting it go.

✱ If you need to scream, cry, or express your anger or tears, do it. Get it out of your body; energetically release it.

✱ Visualize cutting the cord of energy between you and the person or the incident. Say empowering words that resonate with you. For example, *You no longer have power and control over me; I release you with love and light; I mourn what you took from me; I am resilient, I am strong, and I choose to embrace my life.*

✱ Allow the Earth to receive and recycle the energy. It is no longer your burden to carry.

✱ Going back to biblical times, the washing of the hands is a symbolic purification gesture to release connected energy. When you can, wash your hands, take an Epsom salt bath or shower, and wash away any remnants of negative energy to soothe and cleanse your body and spirit.

We attach our feelings to the moment when we were hurt, endowing it with immortality. And we let it assault us every time it comes to mind. It travels with us, sleeps with us, hovers over us while we make love, and broods over us while we die. Our hate does not even have the decency to die when those we hate does—for it is a parasite sucking our blood, not theirs. There is only one remedy for it. Forgiveness!

Lewis B. Smedes, author, *The Art of Forgiving*

MINDFUL MOMENT: *Love Your Body Up*

The skin is the largest organ of the human body. Filled with millions of sensors to protect us from the elements, the skin detects both pain and pleasure. The touch of someone's hand can send chills down our spine or assure a sense of security, allowing us to sense another's energy. Be mindful that your skin is a sensor to the outside world and pay attention to this delicate coating of your body. Love yourself every day by taking an extra two minutes to caress your body with fragrant lotions, healing coconut oil, or creams. Soothing your body by allowing the moisture to seep into the skin, especially after bathing, is healing in itself.

What are your personal rituals for everyday self-care and wellness?

_____

_____

_____

_____

What are your personal goals for the next week?

_____

_____

_____

_____

What are your personal goals for the next month?

_____

_____

_____

_____

What are your personal goals for the next six months?

_____

_____

_____

_____

What are your personal goals for this year?

_____

_____

_____

_____

What are your personal goals for the next five years?

_____

_____

_____

_____

You've always had the power, my dear,
you just had to learn it for yourself.

Glenda, *The Wonderful Wizard of Oz*

Once a woman has forgiven her man,
she must not reheat his sins for breakfast.

Marlene Dietrich, American actress

Chapter Five

HEALING THE HEART

When it comes to matters of the heart, romantic partnerships are most successful when built on a foundation of love and trust. Throughout your passionate journey together, your relationship will experience the highs and lows of life, the beauty of miracles, disappointments, and defining moments you never ever thought would happen to you. Honest communication and forgiveness are key to expressing your feelings with your partner.

While couples may believe the familiar adage that "love means never having to say you're sorry," this can sometimes be an excuse to avoid making amends. Instead, it is always best to apologize if you have caused harm to the person who holds your heart. Next to love, anger is one of the most powerful human emotions we can experience. Being able to release that raging feeling when someone hurts us and choose love for ourselves instead of retaliation, retribution, or hatred is not always easy to do, especially if trauma is involved. It's a conscious practice we must learn on our life's journey of enlightenment.

As Aristotle famously said, "You are what you repeatedly do." If someone says that they are sorry for violating the sacred space of your relationship but continues to be dishonest and misbehave, it will be up to *you* to change that dynamic. The truth is, people do not change unless *they* want to.

In this chapter you will learn that by getting support, maintaining the ritual of your self-care, and believing in the power of yourself, you can choose to heal your heart and either continue your relationship or let it go. When you look back over your life, always choose love for yourself first; it is the only way your partner can fully and completely love you.

I Adore You! Let's Work Together

Anytime there has been a misunderstanding in a relationship that creates hurt feelings, it may often provide an opportunity to learn something about yourself or your partner or shed light on what needs to be strengthened between you two. Here are some mindful ways to connect:

Self-Love + Respect

You must love, honor, and respect yourself first before you can truly love someone else. If you are consistently attending to all your partner's needs while neglecting yours, you will find yourself in an unbalanced relationship and resentment is liable to brew. Always be mindful of what *you* want in your beautiful life; it will only make you happier. The same is true for your partner. If they don't love and respect themselves, how will anyone else?

Communication

The surest step to neutralizing a difficult situation is to communicate with your partner in an unthreatening way. Before jumping to a conclusion and reacting adversely, get the facts. Understanding why, how, or what happened is fundamental to creating a foundation for resolving the issue and repairing the relationship.

Honesty

It is *always* better to tell the truth, no matter the consequences. The truth is always the same, never changes, and will eventually come out no matter how hard someone tries to keep it secret. Admitting the mistake you made can immediately begin to defuse a situation. Honesty also provides the opportunity for trust to heal a fractured relationship.

Couples Therapy

Professional therapy provides a safe place to work out issues and provides guidance as you navigate through a difficult situation to create forgiveness. Covered by most insurance companies, professional counselors support your relationship and can augment the establishment of supportive listening and understanding skills you can use in your relationship.

Moving Forward

After the apologies have been made, both parties in the relationship must be genuine in their willingness to move forward peacefully, leaving an upsetting past incident behind them. Reestablishing trust takes time, space, and patience.

Meaningful Heart-Healing Words

When you simply can't find the right words to sincerely express your feelings, these suggestions may inspire you:

I am sorry. There is no excuse for what I did.

I will be more aware of the choices I am making moving forward.

It was never my intention to cause you pain. I am very sorry.

I'm sorry, I didn't realize I hurt your feelings. Thank you for sharing with me how you feel.

I apologize for hurting your feelings. It was never my intention to do that.

Please forgive me. I really want to learn from this and move forward. Are you open to that?

I made a mistake, and I am truly sorry.

I hope you can find it in your heart to forgive me.

I adore you and would very much like to (work on/mend) our relationship.

I love you endlessly, and I hope my thoughtless words don't define how much I care about you.

The truth is, I was upset about something else entirely; I didn't realize it and I apologize for my behavior.

Yes, your (words/behavior) hurt my feelings, and I'm sorry that what I said caused you such pain.

I am sorry I hurt your feelings, but it's how I feel.

Will you help me understand?

I give you my word.

The Illumination of Clarity: Harnessing Your Intuition

The illumination of clarity is quite literally the "aha moment" when you have that conscious realization, or a download of information suddenly pops into your head. Your intuition is a survival skill instinct that everyone is born with—trust it. One of your senses, intuition, must be exercised like a muscle every day. It is your ability to sense when something isn't right about a person or situation. Pay attention to those "red flags" you pick up; they could save your life.

Surrounding forgiveness, having the intuitive ability for a deeper understanding of why someone behaved the way they did, opens up the space for healing. For example, if someone is constantly criticizing you, step back and consider if that person is jealous or insecure or in some kind of pain. Concentrating on these little moments of clarity must become daily routines of personal awareness so you can be a light for yourself.

When you empathize with a person's hurt versus the pain they've caused as a result of that hurt, forgiveness can be found.

Tyler Henry, American clairvoyant

Unacceptable Behavior in a Romantic Relationship

When you enter into a partnership with someone you love, you believe your devotion to each other will blissfully sail through the storms of life. After all, you both vowed to love each other "in sickness and in health." Unfortunately, relationships are never picture-perfect, and as heartbreaking as it is, every day someone becomes a victim of domestic violence.

No one has the right to make you feel powerless . . . ever. If someone is acting out their anger, their aggression is likely coming from a place within them that needs healing with the help of a professional. Over time, without intervention, verbal or physical abuse can escalate. Be mindful of the following behaviors:

The Bullied Apology

If you are demanding a genuine apology of regret but getting nothing but hurtful and continuous rude and insincere apologies, it might be time to reconsider the future of your partnership. Disrespectful, inconsiderate, and unkind patterns are unhealthy for everyone. While compassion can make excuses for unhealthy conduct from past trauma, violence never feels good, nor is it acceptable. Always remember that people treat you the way you allow them to, and you can choose to leave the relationship. If you are experiencing combative comments in your love life, think about whether this dynamic makes you feel honored and respected.

Physical and Verbal Abuse

When someone refuses to take responsibility for their harmful behavior, you must seek help for your protection and self-preservation.

Abuse and manipulation of any kind are never acceptable, no matter how many times someone apologizes.

Grudges

A grudge is a "persistent feeling of ill will from a past insult or injury." If you have made a mistake and your partner continues to hold the incident over your head, or vice versa, you might want to seek the intervention of a professional therapist to support you.

Begging for Forgiveness

You have apologized repeatedly to your partner, or they have repeatedly said they were sorry and are now begging for your forgiveness. First, one should never beg to be forgiven. If either of you have freely chosen to stay in the relationship, then putting the past behind you is the only way to move forward. Not accepting forgiveness and continuing the grudge is a power play to keep the other person under their control.

Managing Anger

If someone in your life is consistently angry, it is time to have a heart-to-heart with yourself about continuing this relationship. If you choose to end the relationship, very quickly your partner's love for you can turn to jealousy and uncontrollable rage. Acts of rage and impulse can become deadly. It is best not to engage with someone who has gone over the edge in fury. Step back, get yourself to safety, and allow them to calm down. Even if they offer a charming, tearful apology that seems sincere, this person needs professional help beyond what you can do.

Harnessing Anger within Yourself

Anger raises the walls of protection in your body like a defense mechanism, releasing "fight or flight" adrenaline and stress hormones into the body. Perpetuating that heavy energy through your body is like circulating hot liquid, which eventually causes injury to you. Over time, anger will take a hard toll physically and can manifest in medical issues. If someone you love is making you feel this way, or you are continuing to fester over a past incident, consider what that anger is doing to you. Is it worth your health or your life?

Infidelity

Simply put, you can't force someone to love you. If you or your partner have been unfaithful and apologies have been made, you both need to decide if the relationship is worth your love and time to continue it.

Someone gave me advice, they said, "You know not everyone that's hurt you cares." Someone said, "Forgiveness lets you off the hook." Why would you carry that with you if the person doesn't care? Why are you tainting and infecting all the amazing moments that could happen in your life with someone that doesn't care how they hurt you? So how do you figure out how to let that go?

Sandra Bullock, American actress

MINDFUL MOMENT: *Creating Heart Awareness*

Think about how you feel about the person with whom you spend your time or perhaps the rest of your life. How do you feel about your partner?

_____

_____

_____

_____

How do you feel when you are with them?

_____

_____

_____

_____

Do they love and support you in the way that you need?

_____

_____

_____

_____

If you are struggling with forgiveness and you have chosen to continue your relationship after a difficult situation, what do you need to create peace for yourself?

_____

_____

_____

_____

What would your life look like if you moved forward without this person in your life?

_____

_____

_____

_____

Walking Away from a Relationship: It Is *Your* Choice

What if the person who caused the injury has apologized but you have not been able to reestablish trust with them? You saw the bad behavior, the intuitive "red flags," but this time you realized it was unhealthy for you to continue this toxic relationship. Choosing to set a boundary with someone's injurious behavior is *always* a healthy choice, especially if children are involved. Here are some thoughts to support you in this process:

* Thank you so much for apologizing. Yes, I forgive you for (state the issue). After thinking about everything, I realize that this is not a healthy relationship for either of us. I think it would be best for both of us to move on separately.

* I forgive you, but this relationship cannot continue until you get the help and professional support you need to take care of yourself.

* I accept your apology, and I wish you all the best.

Once trust in a relationship has been dishonored, healing the bond between two people can be incredibly strained, sometimes beyond repair. At what point do you choose to walk away when that person consistently causes harm. You are not required to explain why you are discontinuing a relationship with someone, especially if they will retaliate. If your relationship is not working, be honest with yourself and admit it. Never feel you must stay in an unhealthy situation nor try to force or manipulate someone into staying in an uncomfortable partnership with you.

Good Reasons to Walk Away from a Toxic Relationship

Do walk away from a relationship if . . .

* Your partner makes you feel bad or unhappy. It is not a healthy relationship for you.
* The other person continues to hold an offense over your head and can't forgive you (or you can't forgive them).
* They are forcing you to do things you don't want to do, and you are afraid if you don't do what they want, they will become angry.
* Standing up for yourself or setting a boundary creates anger or distance with your partner.
* You or your partner are stalking each other's social media because there is a question of trust.
* They continually lie, and they are likely to be dishonest in other areas as well.
* They are messaging other people on social media and dating sites.
* They make fun of you or put you down over your appearance or intelligence.
* They continue a relationship with a former lover because they are "friends."

❋ You are stalking your partner's digital devices to see who they are texting or talking to or if they are doing this to you.

❋ You are tracking your partner's location without their knowledge, questioning where they go and who they see because they won't tell you.

❋ They are constantly out with their "friends" or on trips, but you are not included.

❋ They have addiction issues you cannot emotionally support.

❋ They have harmed you verbally, mentally, or physically.

Mindful Self-Care: Domestic Violence Emotional Support

If you have decided to move forward following a domestic violence incident, many shelters, support groups, and therapists are available that will lovingly give you the guidance you need. Creating boundaries for yourself and finding forgiveness is a process. Do not be afraid to ask for help, even if that means walking into a police station. There are angels on this Earth. Believe it. The National Domestic Violence Hotline is open 24/7 at 1-800-799-7233 (SAFE) or visit their website at https://www.thehotline.org.

MINDFUL MOMENT: *Music Therapy*

Ancient sages believed in the magical power of music to sooth the mind and heal the body, calling in Apollo, the Greek god of medicine and music. Today, medical researchers at UCLA are proving that music therapy can lift the spirits and improve the mood for children and adults and that some people suffering from memory issues can even remember the words to familiar songs. Create a favorites playlist when you need an immediate pick-me-up or a little mindful relaxation:

What's your power song?

_____

_____

Top Ten Songs on Your Playlist

1. _____

2. _____

3. _____

4. _____

5. _____

6. _____

7. _____

8. _____

9. _____

10. _____

> Music can lift us out of depression or move us to tears—it's a remedy, a tonic, orange juice for the ear. But for many of my neurological patients, music is even more—it can provide access, even when no medication can, to movement, to speech, to life. For them, music is not a luxury, but a necessity.
>
> Dr. Oliver Sacks, British author, *Musicophilia: Tales of Music and the Brain*

Forgiveness is a strange thing. It can sometimes
be easier to forgive our enemies than our friends.
It can be hardest of all to forgive people we love.
Like all of life's important coping skills, the ability to forgive
and the capacity to let go of resentments most
likely take root very early in our lives.

Fred Rogers, American television host, *Mister Rogers*

Chapter Six

NAVIGATING FAMILY BONDS

y far and above, our family relationships create the greatest emotional impact on our hearts and minds. It is in this early home environment that we learn how to behave by observing how we treat one another along with the etiquette of the social graces. That sincere practice of kindness by saying *please, thank you, excuse me, I'm sorry,* and *I forgive you* creates mutual respect and the foundation for living in a civilized world. Implementing the practice of civility in our lives is a common courtesy for respectfully interacting with one another.

While we are blessed to have cherished family members, we are often forced to love, respect, and live with caustic relatives we would never willingly choose to spend time with. To intentionally disregard a family member's bad behavior is unacceptable. It's understandable that no one wants to create more problems by standing up to the offender, but not setting safe boundaries for yourself or failing to step in to protect a child condones and allows the behavior to continue. It is completely unacceptable for everyone involved. An unforgiven moment that happened years ago still carries energetic consequences that have likely festered into resentment and unhealed wounds—all because of not being mindfully respectful of someone else.

In this chapter you will learn how to release and navigate those family bonds to be thoughtful of one another in what we say and do and equally to honor the choices of the people we regard as our "family."

Embracing *Ohana,* Your Family Tribe

The word *family* is commonly defined as a group of one or more parents and their children (or other family members) living together as a unit. Families are a central part of our lives, even though they may be dysfunctional or broken. In Hawaiian, *ohana* is the sanctuary of a person's extended family, which often includes friends and the social groups that have become integral to them. Remember, we choose the people we want to hold sacred in our *family unit*, regardless of whether they are our blood relatives. Surrounding ourselves with those who nurture us with love, while respecting our personal choices and opinions, *are the relationships that are worthy of our emotional investment.* They are our tribe, our people.

Treat Others the Way You Wish to Be Treated

Our interactions with one another reflect our character and integrity, making up the quality of human being that we are. If we ask for forgiveness for our own faulty behavior, we should be equally aware of the *mindfulness of bestowing forgiveness* to someone else.

Teaching Children the Power of Love

As caregivers, we have a responsibility to our children to nurture them, empowering them with love. What we show them by our words and actions becomes a part of the fabric of their lives. If we show love and kindness by living it, that is what they will reflect by the choices and decisions they make sending a ripple effect out into the world. Choosing love for ourselves and for one another, will clearly allow us to be healthier, happier human beings open to forgiveness.

Leave Politics and Religion at the Door

Arguing with family members over their politics or religion can sever relationships permanently, affecting generations. While it's always best to be respectful of another person's beliefs, *agreeing to disagree* is the best advice to "keep the peace," to avoid arguments. No one should apologize for what they feel passionate about, nor should they impose their personal opinions on anyone else. If you feel you can't maintain control in these kinds of situations, graciously remove yourself by not engaging: Step out of the room, change the subject, or don't attend the event. Remember, you can't change others, but you have a choice in how *you* choose to respond.

Mind Your Business

My mother would always say, "It's no longer a secret when you tell someone else." When you repeat someone's business that was shared with you in confidence, you violate that person's trust, and you run the risk of affecting others. Should that person become aware of your betrayal, it could create a break in the relationship or cause a rift in the family dynamic. Best to keep the confidence to yourself and avoid an unnecessary apology. One exception might be that if keeping the secret is detrimental to someone's health and welfare.

Be a Light for Others

We are all human beings on this Earth with equal, undeniable rights, regardless of where we live, what we look like, what we believe, or what language we speak. Being a *light* of respect for others by choosing grace, forgiveness, and compassion can illuminate the darkness for those who propagate fear and hatred.

There are only two days in the year that nothing can be done. One is called yesterday and the other is called tomorrow, so today is the right day to love, believe, do, and mostly live.

Dalai Lama, Tibetan spiritual leader

Meaningful Healing Words for Families

When searching for the right words in pursuit of healing for yourself and your people, here are some thoughts to support you:

I forgive you for everything.

Let's move forward; we both have learned so much from this experience, and I love you.

I can't even put together the words to express how deeply sorry I am to have hurt you and caused you so much pain.

It was never my intention; I was not thinking of the harm I would cause by my actions.

I am just so incredibly sorry.

I am sorry I didn't protect you.

I did not know that happened to you; I am so sorry.

What I did to you was wrong in every way. Thank you for being brave enough to tell me.

I hope one day you will find it in your heart to forgive me.

I want you to know how sorry I am and I apologize for my actions.

I lied and blamed you for it. It's not an excuse, but to provide clarity, I was afraid I would be in trouble; not accepting responsibility only made it worse. I am deeply sorry.

Please forgive me.

I am sorry I called you _____. I was angry, and I was wrong to say it.

I was the one who took your _____. I am so sorry I
lied.

I broke the _____. Please forgive me.

When you can't find the words, simply reaching out and hugging
the other person can revitalize the positive energy between you.

Meaningless Apologies: Just Say You're Sorry

We learned the art of the *meaningless apology* when caregivers
intervened in our childhood quarrels by insisting we say, *I'm sorry*,
thereby ending the feud. The person in authority diminished and
dismissed the incident, creating possible resentment for the injured
individual, especially if there was no effort to truly recover peace. That
learned insincerity from our elders to "just say you're sorry" when
you are not sorry taught us that we don't have to be responsible for
our actions. While some disagreements may seem trivial to adults,
in the eyes of children, they can be monumental events of negative
energy that children hold on to. No matter our age, we can feel the
bitterness of being wronged when followed by an insincere apology,
adding further insult to injury. Following are some dynamics to be
mindful of:

You Never Stand Up for Me

The child that is forced to accept an insincere apology and continue to tolerate the bad behavior of a sibling, parent, or other family
member might experience feelings of powerlessness, resentment, and
anguish possibly choosing similar relationships in their lives. This

could create a situation where a child then carries resentment wishing for the punishment of the offender.

You Don't Believe Me. I Didn't Do Anything!

What about the child who believes that a parent or caregiver sides with the person who created the disturbance and then forces the innocent child to apologize to the offender? This dynamic is present when a parent is at odds with a child and manipulates the other parent to force the child to cooperate by apologizing, even if the child is innocent.

You Always Let Them Get Away with Everything! It's Not Fair!

In this situation, the person who caused the disruption learns that they don't have to be accountable for causing harm to someone else, especially if there are no consequences for their behavior. Their disrespectful actions will likely continue throughout their lives unless respectful boundaries are established.

I Said I Was Sorry!

Most definitely, the apology that is sarcastic and fueled with indignation is worthless. Completely devoid of remorse, the person could hatefully shout an apology and storm off. Some people refuse to admit they are wrong and keep the energy of outrage going, blatantly shifting the blame. In these situations, decide to avoid conflict with toxic people like this. Walk away and set boundaries for self-preservation.

MINDFUL MOMENT: *Meeting Your Younger Self*

Find a quiet place and close your eyes. Breathe in deeply three times. Feel the blanket, grass, or chair beneath your body. Take a moment to reflect on your life, to that one significant event that caused you pain and suffering.

How old are you? Where are you? Who are you with?

_____

_____

_____

_____

_____

_____

See yourself standing next to your younger self in this moment. Now that you are older and wiser, what wisdom can you share with your younger self about the future?

_____

_____

_____

_____

_____

_____

Visualize hugging your younger self with love and acknowledging the trauma, so you may begin the process of release and be free from the pain of the past.

Family Members Who Have Crossed a Boundary

While "finding forgiveness" for aggressive acts committed against you, especially when suffered as a powerless child, is unthinkably appalling, the anguish of living in a mental prison of resentment connected to that person may be worse. It is unlikely that the offender is holding as much pain over the incident as you are. There is no excuse for a family member who has violated you or your personal boundaries —ever. Either verbal, physical, or sexual, this egregious behavior is unconscionable and leaves a lifetime of emotional scarring.

The best way forward is to consider speaking to a mental health professional as part of your self-care plan. With courage and love for yourself, little by little, you can walk the steps to release yourself from the power of traumatic events over your thoughts. In addition to reviewing the forgiveness tools in Chapter 3, here are some thoughts to help you heal:

Why Didn't You Protect Me?

Complicating the situation for the victim is when the offender is a member of the family unit, which allows easy access for the abuse to continue, sometimes with the awareness or suspicions of other relatives. If a parent is allowing another family member to mistreat a child, they are equally responsible and, depending on the situation, should be held accountable.

Telling the Story

The process of "telling the story" of what happened to you is important but only on your terms. While some trauma victims are able to repeat what occurred, others have an excruciating level of difficultly and are fearful for their lives if they tell or report what someone did to them. If a crime has been committed against you and you feel up to taking action, contact your local authorities for further guidance.

Questioning a Victim

It can be retraumatizing to be forced to relive the events of the past. For victims of PTSD, many times the memories are shattered fragments of what they experienced, especially if they had to survive a situation and save their lives. Setting healthy boundaries with a difficult family member is also critical. If people in your world are telling you to "just get along," they are dismissing the behavior of the disruptive person. For your own self-care, if someone is causing you to feel uncomfortable or disrespecting you—you have every right not to be in the presence of that person.

MINDFUL MOMENT: *Family Therapy*

If a family member is intentionally causing disruption and havoc with constant negative behavior, consult your medical provider for a care plan. If your family refuses to participate, you can get the support you need to smartly navigate the family dynamics by speaking to a mental health therapist. If you have not been able to communicate your feelings to this family member about their behavior, write them in the space provided. Give yourself a voice and begin the healing process.

When you behave, say, or do _____, it makes me feel . . .

_____

_____

_____

_____

Releasing False Labels:
My Mother Always Told Me I Was . . .

Despite family members' efforts to be loving to one another, there is a tendency for "labels" to be placed upon us. This can generate a damaging false opinion about ourselves that we mentally carry for years. When we believe, even subconsciously, this label or expectation, it comes with an energetic weight. Sometimes labels are created out of fear, jealousy, or manipulation. For example, when someone, especially a trusted family member, tells you that you are stupid, smart, always causing trouble, you are the favorite, you are such a goody-goody, a fatty, always perfect, liar, jealous, troublemaker, you can't be trusted, or the black sheep of the family, we may believe these statements. It puts us in a box with catastrophic consequences by lowering our expectations of who we are or what we hope to achieve. The truth is, someone else's opinion of us is just that—their opinion. If someone's words don't serve your highest good or empower you, return them to sender because they do not belong to you!

Without forgiveness,
there's no future.

Archbishop Desmond Tutu, Nobel Laureate

MINDFUL MOMENT: *Return to Sender!*

It doesn't matter if the person who "labeled" you is with us on this Earth or in spirit, nor do you need to actually speak to them. What matters is releasing *someone else's words* and redirecting the heavy energy back to the source from which it came. Creating forgiveness here for your own self-care is important so you are not carrying resentment. Here are some forgiving words and actions for your self-care:

When you told me I was _____, I believed it about myself. I realize now that these words do not belong to me, and I am returning them to you, releasing them with forgiveness. I am a loving, kind human being and perfect exactly the way I am.

Visualize the person sitting in front of you. Tell that person that the harmful words they said do not belong to you and that you are returning them.

Write the word on a stone and tell the stone that you are giving away the energy of these harmful words to be recycled back into the Earth with love and light, thereby peacefully releasing it from yourself.

Write a letter expressing your feelings. You can mail it to the person, send it to the universe, burn it, bury it, or destroy it, releasing the energetic connection to you.

Family Separation and Estranged Relatives

An unforgiven situation with an estranged relative can create excruciating circumstances for all members of the family. The holidays and family get-togethers only increase the tension with the person who refuses to be involved or has become unwelcome. The issue here is, why wait until time has taken its toll? The people in our lives are here for only a short time, and we can never go back and repair the missed moments. These examples of intentional damage cause endless frustration for everyone:

Why Won't They Forgive Me?

When someone deliberately refuses to accept your apology, it gives them the power to continue to hold the offense of what you did alive, even though it might have occurred years ago. Continuing to generate that heavy feeling of hatred, however, is only making the unforgiving person unwell. If you have apologized and the family member continues to cause separation, there is likely a deeper issue. For example, if you are more successful in life than your sibling, or maybe they just view you this way, there might be a bit of jealous sibling rivalry. As you really can't heal that issue for another person, respectfully show kindness and compassion. Remember, jealousy is the absence of gratitude.

Choosing Sides?

When someone in the family is unforgiving after a meaningful apology has been made, they might try to secure the support of their position with other family members. Sometimes they may even disallow their children to continue a relationship with other relatives. The damage of this behavior creates a cycle of hatred and is heartbreaking. If this is occurring in your family, take the high road of what is right and just. Decide for yourself whom you want in your life.

You Don't Like My Partner?

The genetic makeup of your tribe can be significantly altered when a new spouse joins the family, or one leaves through divorce. Holidays and get-togethers may be different as allegiances change, personalities clash, and traditions incorporate new ways of celebrating. If the new member is not welcomed, or someone shows their dislike, the family becomes divided, creating a fracture that can be hard to heal. If you have stated that you don't like a family member, particularly one who has married into the family, an avalanche of reactions likely occurred. The best way to heal this is to meaningfully apologize. Then remember the adage: If you have nothing nice to say, don't say anything at all.

MINDFUL MOMENT:
Grounding Yourself—Clarity in a Situation

Rather than impulsively reacting to an incident, take a minute to ground yourself and find clarity in the situation by looking at all perspectives. What is really happening in the moment? Is someone hurt? Jealous? Feeling taken advantage of? How can it be healed?

_____

_____

_____

The Gift of Reconciliation

There is no doubt that when two people in a family come together and reconcile, all is forgiven with love and perhaps a few tears. Letting go of forcing the other person to accept your point of view is also critical here. We all come into every situation colored by the backdrops of our lives and the moments that have defined us. Clearing away the bumps and bruises of life and moving forward in forgiveness is the truest path for peace.

> Let us forgive each other—only then will we live in peace.
>
> Count Lev Nikolayevich Tolstoy, Russian author

MINDFUL MOMENT: *Holiday Communication*

Our digital world has created instantaneous communication, enabling us to see and speak to friends and loved ones no matter where we live. Picking up the phone couldn't be any easier but making a call to heal a situation after years of silence can be difficult. The spirit of the holiday season stimulates people to connect to those broken relationships. If you can't make that phone call, you can always write something thoughtful in a "season's greeting" to heal the divide. Seize the moment of opportunity to reunite with the people who made a difference in your life. Here are a few phrases to get you into the peaceful spirit and break the ice:

* I miss you. Can we get together the next time you are in town?
* I want you to know how much you have meant in my life.
* Regardless of who said what, I love you so much. Let's put the past behind us.
* How are you? I would love to catch up. It has been way too long since we connected.
* I don't even remember what happened, but I do remember how important you are to me.
* I love this picture of us! (Include the picture.)
* Do you remember when _____? Life is too short for us to be apart.
* It feels like we've been separated for a million years. I can't even remember what has kept us apart.

Finding Forgiveness with Substance Abuse

Enduring the reckless behavior of a friend or family member struggling with an addiction is excruciating. While the addict may have apologized relentlessly for their actions that have caused endless anguish, if you are holding on to resentment for what they did or didn't do, it only causes further harm to *you* by continuing that hateful energy.

Recovering from substance abuse is a process, a seemingly endless lifelong struggle, and a daily choice. Here are some ways to support your journey:

Family Mental Support

When you are dealing with an addict in the family, getting the mental support and tools you need are critical to your survival. From confidential in-person or virtual therapy to nationwide support groups like Al-Anon, never be afraid to reach out for your self-care. For more information visit, https://al-anon.org.

Making Peace with the Pain

If you cannot find compassionate forgiveness for the person destroying their life through substance abuse, mindfully decide to put their choices behind you when creating peace for yourself. Although we try to save others from making reckless decisions, it is ultimately that person's life to live and their journey to experience.

MINDFUL MOMENT:
Compassionate Forgiveness with Addiction

According to Sue Kovacs Bellamy, Shamanic Reiki Master, and Teacher of Healing, "When my father drank, he told me to not interfere—he was never going to give it up. Why couldn't he love me, why wouldn't he choose me? It was incredibly frightening to watch him go under that spell of alcohol as it suppressed his spirit, the light of his eyes dimming, witnessing someone else there in his body taking his place. Through a lot of self-work, I was finally able to get to that place of compassionate forgiveness that he was not able to give me what I needed because he was hurting so much from his own life. The illuminating realization that it wasn't about me created a shift and an opportunity to heal not only myself but others in such a unique way. I am so grateful for that." We can't always find a reason for someone's substance abuse but being aware that we are not to blame is important for our healing journey.

Write a letter to the person who has dimmed their spirit through substance abuse. Tell them how it has affected you.

_____

_____

_____

_____

_____

_____

_____

_____

_____

_____

_____

God, grant me the serenity to accept
the things I cannot change, courage to
change the things I can, and wisdom
to know the difference.

Reinhold Niebuhr, American theologian

MINDFUL MOMENT: *Addiction Apology Letter*

An integral healing component of the Alcoholics Anonymous twelve-step program, besides acknowledging surrender to a Higher Power, is self-forgiveness for the choices and decisions we made while walking the destructive road of addiction. Equally important is making amends and apologizing to the people we have harmed. When you can't express in person your sincere remorse for the pain you have caused a family member from substance abuse, writing a letter of apology will allow you the opportunity. It is important to acknowledge the harm your addiction caused and your willingness to make amends by taking responsibility.

Of course, when you send a letter, it releases that *spirit of intention for healing*–for both of you. It is up to the recipient to decide, in their own time, if they wish to create forgiveness, rebuild trust, and continue a relationship with you. If they choose to move forward without you, you have at least taken the healing step of acknowledging regret and asking for forgiveness. Always be mindful that even if you believe a relationship has been shattered beyond repair, meaningfully saying *I'm sorry* is always the right thing to do for everyone involved.

Dear _____,

I am sorry . . .

_____

_____

_____

_____

_____

_____

For more information on Alcoholics Anonymous or for a support group near you visit https://www.aa.org.

Healing LGBTQ Family Dynamics

The personal choice of our sexuality should be just that—*personal.* Whom you have chosen to love is none of anyone's business because the intimacy you share with another human being is sacred.

It often happens that we want to find forgiveness for the family member who refused to accept us or, in retrospect, for the way we negatively reacted to someone's life decisions that separated us. It is important to be mindful of the bravery of the LGBTQ person who steps forward, "coming out," thinking, *If I tell my family how I really feel, will they still love me?*

Family relationships can be severed or fractured for generations, lives destroyed and taken because of someone else's opinion. Here are some loving words to support you as you embrace one another:

* ❋ Thank you for trusting me.
* ❋ I hope you can find it in your heart to forgive me for not respecting your decisions.
* ❋ I love you and want to move forward together.
* ❋ I want you to feel open to express your authentic self.
* ❋ I am so proud of you, no matter whom you love.
* ❋ Please give me time to learn, adjust, and accept.
* ❋ I will never ever stop loving and supporting you.
* ❋ I ask you to forgive me for reacting in such a way as to make you feel alienated or unloved.
* ❋ Why didn't you tell me sooner? Did you think I would stop loving you? Never.
* ❋ I can't express how much I regret my reaction; please forgive me.
* ❋ It took so much bravery for you to share this with me.
* ❋ I love you.

MINDFUL MOMENT: *Opening Your Heart*

The most valuable support we can provide is to really listen and respect the choices of the people we adore in our lives. Here are several questions to think about when you are opening your heart:

What is more important to you, your child or family member's genuine happiness in loving someone or the negative judgment of someone else?

_____

_____

_____

_____

_____

_____

_____

How deeply do you hold value in the opinion of others regarding the thoughts and feelings of your child or family member? Is it worth losing that child or family member in your life?

_____

_____

_____

_____

_____

_____

_____

What can you do to be an inspiration of healing for someone else?

_____

_____

_____

_____

_____

_____

_____

It's not anyone's journey; it's yours.
Write your brave and beautiful story.

Two persons cannot long be friends
if they cannot forgive each other's little failings.

Jean De La Bruyère, French philosopher

Chapter Seven

CHOOSING YOUR COMPANY OF FRIENDS

True friends are blessings that enrich and sweeten our lives. Some walk with us for a short time while others stand by our side for a lifetime. We often choose our dearest friends simply because of the sparkly way they make us feel. The essence of their spirit, their adventures, or similar interests create a common bond. We are attracted to them and spend time together sharing our deepest secrets, hopeful dreams, and darkest fears. They become an integral part of the fabric of our lives—our *chosen family*. Some soul connections go so deep that we know what the other is thinking and embrace the knowledge that they are our *person*.

There is no doubt that all relationships will experience challenges and difficulties that will determine the course of the friendship. People evolve and change, make different life choices, and move in opposite directions. We become separated by time, space, opportunities, or a new romance that might take our place, hurting us to our core. The divide is created, silence occurs, and the growing pains of life move forward. For the relationship to thrive, it must grow and become resilient to change.

When you are upset and focusing on a singular moment of your friendship, remember your history together and the essence of what created that magical spark between you in the first place. Unfortunately, for some relationships, you must choose to say goodbye because it is the best decision for you.

In this chapter, you will learn how to be mindfully aware of treasuring the friendships that you hold near and dear.

To Thine Own Self Be True: Loving Yourself First

The ability to have meaningful relationships begins with how you love and honor *yourself*. You are responsible for your happiness and self-worth. If you surround yourself with unhappy people, take a step back and consider why you are gravitating toward this type of personality. What are you getting out of the relationship? If someone is always negative around you, then that is the energy you will absorb.

While everyone will experience trials and tribulations, some people are always complaining instead of counting their blessings. Surrounding yourself with positive people will cast that light of inspiration in your life. If you feel someone is pulling you down, it is absolutely alright to set a healthy boundary and create space. Always choose to love yourself and consider what is best for you.

MINDFUL MOMENT:
Important Qualities in a Friendship

Always remember, "To have a friend, you must be a friend." When choosing the friends you keep in your life, being mindful of the qualities that are important to you in a relationship is essential. Here are some examples:

honesty	love	trust
integrity	kindness	support
compassion	respect	honor

What qualities do you value that you would like in a friendship?

_____

_____

_____

_____

_____

_____

_____

_____

_____

_____

_____

_____

You're My Best Friend—I Want You in My Life!

There are varying degrees of friendships across our lives. Some friends are like angels, always providing support through a difficult time while others may be acquaintances we nod to or "like" on social media. When it comes down to it, having one person you know that will show up for you in a moment of crisis is a blessing.

Before walking away from a meaningful friendship, step back and reflect on the importance of this person to you. Communicating and expressing your gratitude for their support through tough times is a positive way to avoid the hurt feelings of not being appreciated. Here are some ideas to say, text, post, write, and remember:

✳ Thank you for always being there for me!

✳ You are my ride or die!

✳ You are my partner in crime.

✳ I know I can call you and you'll come.

✳ Thank you for being my friend!

✳ You are the best!

✳ You rock!

✳ I have no words—thank you for making my day!

✳ I have so much respect for your opinion.

✳ I love you and support you!

Many people will walk in and out of
your life, but only true friends will
leave footprints in your heart.

Eleanor Roosevelt, American First Lady

You Have to *Be* a Friend to Have a Friend!

One-sided friendships are those relationships where one person is always giving to the other without reciprocating that same level of kindness, love, and attention. If the conversations are always about the other person, who never asks how you are, or on the contrary you are uninterested in them, but you keep talking about yourself—it's not a healthy relationship. One person is constantly giving and the other always receiving. The giving person will eventually feel taken advantage of and might become resentful. Having the awareness of being treated like this in a friendship can help you alter your perspective about whether you want to continue it.

We *choose* our friends. We give to them because we want to, but if they continually fail to reciprocate after we have communicated our feelings, it's your choice to keep on giving or reevaluate the relationship. Move on from someone who drains your time and energy. They will quickly latch on to someone else to meet their needs. If you want to keep this person in your life, it would be best to change your expectations.

Actions Speak Louder Than Words: Keeping Friends and Letting Go

Life is too short to maintain relationships that don't have your best interests at heart. Sometimes, we like someone so much that we overlook behavior that isn't healthy for us, and we find ourselves making needless apologies just to stay friends. Unfortunately, it's those ignored intuitive "red flags" that lead to the end of a relationship. If you are walking on eggshells around your bestie, take a minute to reflect on the dynamic of your relationship. There are billions of beautiful people who would treasure you as their friend.

Remember, to have forgiveness for yourself as well as compassion for your friend. Think twice about the "friends" that might create negative energy by exhibiting some of these behaviors:

unforgiving	jealous	gossiping
blaming	hurtful	borrows without returning
dishonest	failing to show up	talks behind your back
controlling	fighting	makes unhealthy life choices
manipulative	toxic behavior	expects you to pay
critical of you	always angry	using you to get something

Speaking Your Truth: Communicating Hurt Feelings

The mistake has been made; the damage is done. Where do you go from here? Do you try to mend the relationship or release it entirely? Once you have stubbornly stopped speaking to each other, the silence is deafening. The love between friends can quickly turn to hate when we feel betrayed. Everything around us shifts: the weekend plans, texts, FaceTimes, or just having that special person who was a daily part of your life. Their absence is similar to the heartbreak of grief.

Take the Time and Space You Need to Calm Down

When we are in a heightened state of emotion, we say and do things we would not normally say or do in a rational state of mind. Rather than engage when you feel this way, take a day or two to allow everyone the grace to calm down and then reassess.

Speak to Each Other

It's always better to hear someone's voice, video chat, or meet in person if possible. Avoid texting as it can be misinterpreted.

I Felt...

Communicating how you feel is important. Rather than saying, "You made me feel . . ." which may come across like an accusation, take responsibility for your feelings by not making someone else responsible for them. Instead, say, "I felt . . ." It will support the other person's ability to hear what you are saying. Consider these examples when communicating:

I felt so left out.   I felt hurt when you said _____.
I didn't feel included.   When this happened, I felt _____.

Avoid People Pleasing

If you are really not sorry for something but you say you are to keep the peace and maintain your friendship, stop and consider why you are not standing up for yourself and giving your power away. Some friends thrive on creating drama and pulling the focus to themselves.

I Feel You Aren't Making Time for Me

No matter how much you want to be friends with someone, if they consistently don't make plans or don't respond to your calls, emails, or texts, it might be that they no longer wish to continue the relationship, or they might view the friendship differently than you do. While you might have hurt feelings because the person you thought was your friend doesn't reciprocate, you have to accept it. You can't control someone else's feelings.

Send a "Making Amends" Card

There is something personal about sending a card to a friend in the mail, no matter how far apart you are. It carries a different feeling than an email or text because it is in your handwriting. Include a nice foil-wrapped tea bag and write, "Let's meet for tea" in person or via video chat. If flowers are more appropriate for an apology, a pretty packet of seeds is a unique and thoughtful token to bridge a gap to "grow" a new foundation for a relationship.

MINDFUL MOMENT: *The Healing Ritual of Tea*

For thousands of years, across continents and cultures, the healing properties of tea have been widely known. As magical elixirs, meditative medicine, or simply nourishment for the body, tea has the unique characteristic to bring people together and calm the soul. For your mindful self-care moment, or to create a meaningful space to communicate with a friend, ancient sages say, "There is nothing that a cup of tea can't solve." Whether you choose to restore your relationship or to move forward by releasing each other, the ritual of sitting together, pouring the hot water over the leaves, and waiting patiently as the tea brews creates the opportunity for healing and communication.

If you could have a cup of tea with anyone, who would it be and what would you want to say to them?

_____

_____

_____

_____

_____

Meaningful Heartfelt Words for Friendships

When you want to reach out and touch someone's heart to let them know you care, here are some heartfelt words to bridge the distance:

While we may be separated, I want you to know that of all the people I have walked through this life with, it is your friendship I treasure most.

I will love and adore you always, regardless of this moment that has put us on a different journey.

I miss your friendship in my life.

If you need me, I will always be here.

I am so sorry I wasn't there for you.

I apologize for the way I behaved and treated you.

I regret the distance between us and wish I could go back. Please know I miss you.

MINDFUL MOMENT: *Self-Care Awareness*

Your time is valuable. Make sure to prioritize and put your energy, thoughts, and feelings toward friendships that create abundance in your life. Close your eyes, put your hands on your chest, and take three deep breaths.

How am I feeling today? Why am I feeling this way?

_____

_____

_____

_____

_____

What can I do to take care of myself today?

_____

_____

_____

_____

What am I putting my energy toward? Is it worth my time and attention?

_____

_____

_____

_____

_____

Breaking Up Is Hard to Do: Respectfully Releasing a Relationship

There is never an easy way to end a relationship with someone, especially when you have shared so many memories. If you are choosing to move forward in your life, keep these insights in mind:

Social Media

When you are at odds with each other, or the relationship is beyond repair, avoid posting your negativity online. Remember, you were once friends. Subtweeting to intentionally cause harm to someone else is never a good idea. Putting hurtful words out into the universe, hoping the person might see and react to them, doesn't do you any good but sends more ill will your way.

Secrets and Gossip

Instead of repeating information that was shared with you in sacred confidence, keep it to yourself. Breaking someone's trust is a violation. Rather than intentionally creating negativity to harness hard feelings, do something nice for yourself instead.

Path of Life

It will happen somewhere along in your life that you will bump into the person you are no longer friends with. You have a *choice* to take the high road of being cordial or a path of using negative energy in the form of body language, words, or facial expressions. Of course, when we see someone who has caused us suffering, we have a visceral reaction. Take a moment to breathe and leave the past behind you. It is the single most powerful action you can take for yourself.

MINDFUL MOMENT: *Self-Care in Friendships*

Being mindfully aware of our interconnectedness in a relationship is important. Think for a moment about a relationship you treasured either in the past or at present. What are those things that you held or continue to hold near to your heart?

_____

_____

_____

_____

How do you feel when you think of that person?

_____

_____

_____

Do you feel your friend honors and respects you? Or do you feel you give up part of yourself?

_____

_____

_____

Is there any moment in your relationship you wish you had been forgiving or asked to be forgiven? Write about it.

_____

_____

_____

Looking back, what do you wish you had done?

_____

_____

_____

_____

Write a letter to that friend and express how you feel. It is important to move this energy out of your heart and mind. Release the letter by sending it, burning it, burying it, or releasing it however you choose; it is the act of emotional release that is key.

_____

_____

_____

_____

Getting over a painful
experience is much like
crossing monkey bars. You have
to let go at some point to
move forward.

C. S. Lewis, British writer

I'm still someone who is the first to
apologize when I'm wrong. But I think I'm better
at standing up for myself when I've been wronged.
So, that's something that I think
also comes with growing up.

Taylor Swift, American singer and songwriter

Chapter Eight
STICKS, STONES, AND THE SCHOOLYARD

During the early years of our education, we are forced to interact with others with whom we might never willingly choose to have a relationship. We must learn to get along and stand up for ourselves or be crushed by the thoughtless words of the bullies that called us names we remember for a lifetime. Deeply hurtful moments as a child may define us if we *choose* to let them.

Unless our children communicate what is happening in their lives, we aren't always aware of how to support them as they navigate challenges with other children, as well as their teachers, staff, and coaches. While some parents let their kids just figure it out for themselves, being a role model and teaching our children how to recover from adversity and how to be resilient through forgiveness provides the best course of action. Mistakes will happen, fights will occur, and feelings will be hurt, but this is how we learn to do it better, and forgiveness is part of the package. My mother always said, "If you don't go through life without any difficulties, you will never learn to be resilient." We can't fight our kids' battles, but we can teach what's right from wrong, so they are fully prepared to stand up for themselves with confidence and knowledge instead of revenge. Having healthy, happy children that thrive in making the world a better place is something we all want. In this chapter you will learn how to mindfully forgive past hurtful moments, navigate bullies, and embrace the forgiveness tools needed to navigate the schoolyard.

How to Help Your Child Navigate Forgiveness

We are born into this world as pure spirits, *all of us equal.* It is our set of life circumstances, the family we become a part of, where we live in the world, and the people we meet along the way that mold us into the person we become. As we grow and attend school, we are joined in the classroom with others of diverse backgrounds, different languages, and various religious beliefs. When accidents happen or mistakes are made, how we *choose* to respond is colored by this melting pot of conditions that make up who we are in that exact moment.

Model Forgiveness at Home

The best way to teach our children about forgiveness is to share it with others and return it to ourselves with grace. Things are going to happen in our lives that are completely unfair, but it is how we choose to respond that makes the difference for our personal mental health. When our children witness our choice of moving forward in peace instead of anger, we positively influence them and the generations to follow.

Compassion

Sometimes, when a child misbehaves at school, it's because of an extenuating circumstance in their life, of which you may know nothing about—nor is it your problem to solve. Whether they may have said or done something harmful to someone else, it is likely that this child might feel powerless in their situation. It's never an excuse for poor behavior but having the light of compassion can help you shift your child toward creating forgiveness and compassion.

Getting to the Heart of the Matter

Before reacting, step back and look at what is at the heart of the situation. Is it jealously? Feeling left out? Were hurtful words used as weapons? Getting clarity regarding a conflict and talking it out can help create an understanding that promotes healing.

Forgiving Someone Who's Not Sorry

When someone refuses to apologize for intentionally causing harm, or gives you an insincere "fake apology," it speaks to the kind of person they are. For a purehearted child, this is a moment of clarity, when they will need to rise up with wisdom, put on their "civility suit," and choose love for themselves to peacefully put the matter behind them.

Embracing Apologies and Forgiveness . . . and Moving On

We learned in Chapter 2 and Chapter 3 how to apologize and how to create forgiveness. No matter one's age, the concepts apply. In the classroom, on the playground, or beyond, communicating sound advice to our children can help support their confidence.

Agree to Disagree

You are unique. How you look at something through your life lens is completely different from someone else. When an event occurs, each of you will interpret what happened through a colored lens of perception, which may be different from what actually occurred. When settling something, sometimes it's best to encourage your child to always take the high road by being a peacemaker and leaving the past behind them.

Not Everyone Wants to Be Your Friend

That's just the way it is sometimes when children are forced together in the classroom. Having a network of friends outside of school helps create the best friends. However, regardless of whether "friends" hang out in the classroom or after-school, in order to work well together we must practice a level of civility, respect, and cooperation toward one another.

Giving the Stink Eye

Apologies have been made, yet one person continues to throw negativity your way in the form of twisted facial expressions like the wide-eyed "stink eye." Meant to be menacing, it can come across as threatening. Why harness all that hatred toward someone? You are only hurting yourself in doing so. Shift the focus to yourself.

Always let your conscience
be your guide.

The Blue Fairy, *Pinocchio* by Carlo Collodi

Standing Up for Yourself

Forgiving someone for a mistake never means they have permission to cause you additional harm in any form. It also doesn't mean that you must be their friend or continue the relationship. Setting a boundary is completely appropriate.

Apology Awareness

A good example of leadership in a difficult situation is showing our children we are strong by taking responsibility and diffusing hurt feelings to mend relationships. When another parent is outraged that no one was considerate enough to acknowledge the harm their child endured, step up and diffuse the anger. Saying something like "I am so sorry for what happened between our children. Please let us know how we can rectify the (situation/work together) to create peace." Of course, the ideal situation is when children take responsibility for themselves and meaningfully apologize to one another.

Power of Positivity: Embracing Compliments

What you believe about yourself influences every choice and decision you make. As parents, guardians, and educators, not only is it important to praise the children we care for but to bestow that awareness of love and gratitude on ourselves. Just acknowledging small moments with appreciation will boost confidence. Say, text, or even post empowering words on your bathroom mirror and let the power of positivity flow! For example, *You are so …*

brave	wise	positive	loyal
intelligent	creative	poised	confident
talented	courageous	amazing	self-reliant
smart	powerful	loved	

MINDFUL MOMENT: *Connecting to Your Child*

When our children attend school, they are learning not only how to read and write but also how to navigate interpersonal relationships. Making sure we maintain our connection to them is critical to loving and supporting them throughout their young years, especially when our own life experiences involving forgiveness might provide the healing advice they need to move forward.

When driving our children to school, sharing a meal, or saying good night, we have the opportunity to provide a safe space and create a mindful moment for them to reflect. Taking inspiration from my dear friend LeeAnn Kreischer, here are some questions to keep in mind as we listen to their hearts:

How was your day?

_____

_____

_____

_____

_____

What was the best part of your day today?

_____

_____

_____

_____

_____

_____

What was the worst thing that happened today?

_____

_____

_____

_____

_____

How did that make you feel?

_____

_____

_____

_____

_____

What are you grateful for?

_____

_____

_____

_____

_____

Forgive your enemy,
but do not mistake him
for a friend.

Paulo Coelho, Brazilian novelist

The Mindfulness Treasure Box: Coping Skills

One of the best ways to help manage stress, panic, or anxiety, especially after a traumatic event, is to have an arsenal of easy to access coping skills to create a shift of perspective. Creating a Mindfulness Treasure Box for yourself or someone you care for is truly an endless gift. Choose a box of any kind and decorate it with pictures, empowering words, stickers, or even bedazzle it. Then fill your box with things you love, activities you can do, or phrases that lift you up and bring you joy. Evoking your senses of sound, smell, taste, sight, and touch creates a calming effect. Include a journal to express your feelings in this moment. Ask yourself, *What do I love?* And feel that connection of how it changes you, bringing you into this moment of comfort. As my mother always said, "This too shall pass." Here are a few ideas and activity notes to put into your box:

hot chocolate packet	snuggle with a pet
tea bag	go for a walk or run
favorite candy	bike ride
crayons and paper	hot bubble bath
fragrant candle	bake cookies
bath oil	call a friend
aromatherapy oil	favorite song
favorite photo	meditate
nature sounds playlist	ground yourself
empowering words	

What other items or activities would you like to include?

_____

_____

_____

MINDFUL MOMENT: *Releasing Sticks and Stones*

There is no doubt that there is "truth in jest," and when someone teases you their words can hurt for years to come. When a bully picks on someone, calling them "names," they are trying to empower *themselves* through intimidation. They are creating havoc because they feel powerless and are likely insecure about themselves.

When you look back on a moment of injured feelings, try to view it through the lens of compassion, not only for yourself, but also for the miserable bully. How did that person get so low in their life that they have to harm someone else? If you can imagine the bully in front of you, tell them that their words don't belong to you, and you are returning them. You can write them down and then release them back by any method that feels right: mailing, shredding, burying, burning, or even writing them on a rock and putting it in nature. The best way to handle a bully is to ignore them, but if their harassing behavior continues, report what's going on to the school authorities. While some parents don't want to create a problem, bullies often get stronger when they get away with bad behavior.

The bully only has power because you are hurt by what he says or does. If you are not hurt, he has no power. You are not what they say you are. You have to know who you are . . . If I start insulting you in another language you feel nothing . . . they don't mean anything to you because it's you who puts the meaning to it. Me, I know what it means but it doesn't matter how hard I screamed it to you, you will start laughing. Take their words, take away the value of the words and drop them to the floor. If you take that away they fall to the ground. They never get to touch you. They are nothing.

Salma Hayek, Mexican American actress and producer

Mental Health Training in Schools

Children using digital tools have access to an excess amount of unfiltered information. With a few words, they can search for ways to retaliate when someone has caused them harm or compare themselves to others on social media. Counting their blessings and being aware of forgiveness at home should also be modeled in the classroom with teachers, staff, and coaches. By shining a light on mental health early on, we can empower our children. The following are a few ideas to ignite the spark in your community:

Counselors

Every school should have a mental health counselor on staff for students to be able to communicate what's going on in their lives and to share their concerns. This is an active resource for conflict resolution. If the school can't have one on-site, there is no reason the school can't provide a remote therapist in a virtual format for students to access while maintaining their right to privacy.

Anxiety and Panic Attacks

We all react to crises, trauma, and embarrassing situations differently. Some of us are sensitive, and hurtful words and judgment of others can cause anxiety or panic attacks—some that last for days. Panic attacks can be so debilitating that thoughts of suicide—to escape the excruciating pain—are common. Teaching our children what a panic attack is, showing them mindful tools for self-care, and shifting their perspective can save their lives.

Conflict Resolution

Every child should be aware of how to solve a problem using some method of conflict resolution that's age appropriate. Listening to others' perspectives, allowing everyone the ability to speak, and prioritizing resolving the conflict without pointing fingers at who's wrong and who's right, and then moving forward in peace.

Forgiveness Education

Creating a mindful awareness of forgiveness for our children is a gift they will carry forever. Remember, "mindfully forgiving" someone is *your* mental decision to consciously choose to disempower resentment by energetically releasing the incident from your thoughts, rendering it powerless, and actively moving toward inner peace for your own happiness and healing.

Zero-Tolerance Policy

Anti-bully policies are often part of an academic contract signed by parents and students at the beginning of the school year . . . and then forgotten. The real issue is that many students don't recognize that they are bullying, forgetting what the rules are and that they apply to *everyone*. Posting the policy where students and parents can be regularly reminded of civility and kindness to one another can support a positive environment.

Sticks and stones may break
my bones, but names will
never harm me.

Proverb

Humiliation, Anxiety Attacks, and Suicide

Words carry intense energy that stick, affecting us deeply. What can seem like overwhelming humiliation can trigger excruciating anxiety that feels uncontrollable. For any child to escape, to choose a way out by taking their own life is a tragically devastating decision. Every child should be aware of what a panic attack feels like and have access to mental health tools to manage this crippling stress. They must learn to understand that what is happening in this difficult moment will pass, our classmates and teachers—it is all temporary. From sexual identity, family crises, relationship issues, school performance, and conflict, there are accessible resources just a click or call away. For youth support contact https://suicidepreventionlifeline.org/help-yourself/youth/.

Momma Drama: Dealing with Parents and Other People's Kids

When our children go to school it's an exciting time to forge new relationships, creating a supportive community with other parents. Like our children, we too must interact with people with whom we might never choose as friends. As this community of school parents may stay together for many years, navigating issues of unresolved disputes is essential so they are not carried forward. When a parent, teacher, coach, or other student crosses a boundary, creating an issue, what active step of resolution you take toward healing a situation will determine the outcome. Keep these adages in mind when steering through potential problems on the playground:

Mind Your Own Business

If it's not happening under your roof, with your child, or you didn't see it happen, mind your own business and avoid getting involved in unnecessary drama that doesn't belong to you.

Those Who Gossip to You, Gossip About You

Anyone who talks about someone else will eventually talk about you too. Remember, if you send a text about someone, it can be easily shared with others.

Actions Speak Louder Than Words

Observe how someone treats another person because one day they will treat you the same way. It is a sign of their character. Rather than call someone out in a lie, be mindful of how you interact with them. Sages say, "Once someone shows you who they are, believe it, the *first* time."

Pay Attention to the Red Flags

Intuition is one of our superpower senses that can save our life. If you feel uneasy about someone or something, listen to it and trust it.

Judge Not, Lest You Be Judged

If you are judging another parent and don't agree with the choices they are making for themselves or their children, step back. Just because you would do something differently doesn't mean anyone's parenting style is wrong. Focus on *your life* and the family under your roof.

Loose Lips Sink Ships

Happy hour with other parents provides the time and space to exchange secrets and overshare information you would not otherwise have divulged had you not had those cocktails. If you are concerned you might "spill the beans" or "spill the tea"—stick to a coffee.

Neither a Friend nor Enemy Be

If you have chosen not to be friends with another parent, rather than communicating your feelings by words or behavior, simply be indifferent. You may not like someone, but you need to get along with them and have a certain sense of civility. Do your best to be cordial. Your children are watching everything you do.

Do the Right Thing

Always choose the path that is honorable. If you made a mistake, trust that it is part of the human experience. Lesson learned, say you are sorry, make your amends, and move on.

Meaningful Healing Words for Parents on the Schoolyard

During our children's school years, we frequently interact with other parents and school staff daily. Naturally, life events occur that might affect our communication, and when we realize we took our feelings out on someone else, apologies are in order. When you have to clear the air and take the high road to smooth a situation over, take the uncomfortable energy out by diffusing the situation. Here are some words to support you:

I think we had a misunderstanding. If I (said anything/did something) to offend you, I apologize.

I'm so sorry, I think we got off on the wrong foot.

I overreacted, and I am sorry about that. I would love to meet for coffee one day after drop-off.

I want to apologize if I came across rudely. There was so much going on around me, and I felt overwhelmed at that moment.

I would love to set up a time to connect with you about what is going on at school with our kids.

I saw that!

Karma

MINDFUL MOMENT: *Releasing a Balloon to God*

When my sister was a little girl, she was so upset by the names another girl was calling her at school that she refused to go. My mother was beside herself, telling her that the names this girl was saying were completely untrue. But as a child, my sister didn't understand how to release the harm. My mom got a bright red helium balloon and handed her a marker. "Write on that balloon what she's calling you, and let's go out and let that balloon go up to God. He'll take care of it." She did just that. The next day at school, the bully's words meant nothing. My sister knew and fully believed the matter was now in God's hands.

What would you write on your balloon to release up into the heavens?

_____

_____

_____

_____

_____

_____

_____

_____

_____

_____

Life is too short to wake up in the morning with regrets.
So love the people who treat you right, forgive the ones who
don't, and believe that everything happens for a reason.
If you get the chance, take it. If it changes your life, let it.
Nobody said it would be easy, they just promised
it would be worth it.

Author Unknown

What it taught me was forgiveness.
It taught me that when people present themselves
in a certain way, there's probably some back story or
issue or reason for the way that they are . . . And a lot of times,
it's about something that's completely out of their control.

Denzel Washington, Academy Award winner

Chapter Nine

WORKING DAY AND NIGHT

Unless you were born with a fairy godmother, you must have a source of income to provide for yourself and your family. Whether your career is in a corporate setting, a small shop, or remote, ethical professional behavior must *always* be your standard.

As we often spend so much time pursuing our careers, many of our coworkers become our dearest friends, our "work families," or our romantic partners. When respectful conduct is crossed with insensitive actions by a company or a coworker, an energetic divide is created, and complaints are sure to follow. How an individual or business responds to a grievance—with an apology followed by appropriate disciplinary action if appropriate—will influence the outcome of the solution.

Actively cultivating a workplace culture of mutual respect among employees and customers should be the standard way every company operates. Doing so creates the expectation of how people should interact with one another. Getting ahead of potential issues by laying the foundation of appropriate behavior, harassment training tools, and a system of confidentially reporting incidents will support appropriate manners in the workplace. In this chapter you will learn how to create a culture of professional manners in the workplace, how to properly apologize, and how to move forward.

Creating a Culture of Professional Manners

One of the best ways to avoid a misunderstanding is to practice professional manners—no matter what your position is. Being mindful of our behavior and taking responsibility for what we say and do is the best way to maintain integrity. Keep these manners in mind when you interact with your coworkers and the public:

Always Say "Please" and "Thank You"

The last complaint you want to apologize for is because you didn't acknowledge someone with respect for their work or ask them nicely to do something. Some people might perceive a request to do something as a demand if it's not preceded by "please." Kindness and courtesy go a long way toward feeling appreciated for the work you do.

Communicate Respectfully

There is no place in a work environment to be disrespectful or demeaning to anyone ever. If someone is not performing their job appropriately, have a conversation with them about what your expectations are. Being abusive verbally or through e-mail or text will only open the door to your departure. This behavior is not acceptable in any environment. Apologizing after the incident may smooth the situation, but *you* may be asked to leave your position. If you are feeling upset over your interactions with someone else, step away, calm down, and get clarity on the situation, then report what's happening to your human resources team.

Harassment Prevention

Most corporate cultures insist on appropriate personal behavior in the workplace to protect the family of employees. Besides, it's the law and protection of our civil rights. Office romances and unwanted sexual advances are typically grounds for termination. When inappropriate behavior is reported, but management fails to protect their team members, it can create a legal situation. Sexual harassment training and laying down the expectations of appropriate behavior for everyone should be mandatory *before* an unfortunate situation occurs. If your workplace doesn't offer training, free training videos on appropriate employee behavior in the workplace are available online.

Excuse Me

It goes without saying that when you cough or sneeze, always cover your mouth to prevent spreading sickness. Saying "excuse me" is a form of asking for forgiveness and is a matter of courtesy. This extends to unexpected bodily functions.

Cultural Awareness

When meeting with people from other countries, it's advisable to research their culture's business customs. For example, if you are meeting with a foreign dignitary, it may not be appropriate to introduce them by their first name. Rather than lose a potential opportunity and apologize for the disrespect, inquire what is the expected custom for the business interaction. Tip: The Protocol School of Washington is an excellent resource for in-person and online training in professional etiquette for our global marketplace.

Professional Correspondence

Knowing how to properly send business communication is critical to a company's success. Rather than apologize for a company oversight, get the connection right. How a conversation begins often has a huge impact on how the subsequent conversation goes. Author Robert Hickey's book, *Honor & Respect: The Official Guide to Names, Titles, and Forms of Address*, is an excellent guide to getting names, titles, and forms of address correct on professional and social correspondence.

No matter what the circumstances are, it is best to pursue behavior that is above reproach, because then you will be respected for your actions.

Rosa Parks, American civil rights activist

How to Say "Sorry" in Business

There is likely not a single person who has not made a mistake that required an apology in the journey of their career. Whether it's a missed meeting, confusion, or a lapse in judgment, we all have days when we didn't get it right. Some people might wholeheartedly acknowledge the error while others may deflect responsibility, shrugging their shoulders and shifting the blame to someone else. It takes a lot of character to rise to the occasion and admit your mistake. It's also the surest route to take if you want to succeed in your career. In addition to the information in Chapter 2, be mindful of the following phrases when apologies are in order:

My Apologies for the Miscommunication

If you made the mistake, it will help to resolve it by immediately acknowledging the confusion and your willingness to correct it.

I'm Sorry We Got Off on the Wrong Foot; Let's Set Something Up to Reconnect

If you made an error when interacting with someone, take the negative energy out of it and reestablish the connection if possible.

Let's Put This Behind Us

This is the best position to take if you have come to terms with the disagreement and sort out a resolution. You never know when you will cross paths with someone in life and have to work with them or do business again. Taking the high road of integrity is always the smart choice for your peace of mind.

Well, I'm Sorry You Feel That Way

If you are shrugging your shoulders and saying "sorry" in an intentionally sarcastic way, this phrase comes across as if you are just apologizing without taking any responsibility. However, if the other person is being unreasonable and you have done your best to reconcile the relationship, it might be best to end the connection . . . without being sarcastic.

I'm Sorry I'm Late!

Being punctual in the personal and business arena is critical to your success. Arriving on time for an appointment, meal, or meeting is good manners and shows that you respect the other person's valuable time. Being a few minutes early is even better, as it allows you to pause and collect yourself, in order to prepare for the meeting. Of course, there are always valid reasons why you might be late, from traffic to family conflicts; delays will happen. Being courteous to the other person waiting for you, with a sincere apology, will help soothe the situation, especially when time is money. Keep these thoughts in mind when planning your day:

If You Arrive Late

An immediate sincere apology is necessary. If you are just a few minutes late, a simple apology without elaborating is completely appropriate. When you are unreasonably late, an explanation should accompany your apology.

If You Know You Will Be Late for an Appointment or Meeting

Contact the other party to let them know that you are running late. If your timing is such that you need to reschedule, or they can no longer accommodate you in their day, the earlier you communicate the better.

If You Are Running Late to a Lunch or Dinner

Never assume that being more than five minutes late is acceptable, or that the person you're meeting doesn't care if you arrive exactly on time or not. If you can't contact the person on their mobile device, call the restaurant and ask that they let the person waiting for you know.

If You Are Consistently Late

Always running late, regardless of the reason, is disrespectful to everyone waiting for you, and it might be grounds for termination. It also creates resentment with your employer and coworkers who are forced to cover your position. Plan to leave fifteen minutes early so you always arrive on time.

How to Move Forward *After* the Professional Apology

Unless there has been an egregious, unrecoverable incident in an employee's performance or behavior, most companies ensure their human resources team follows a plan of oral and written warnings before the employee is placed on suspension or terminated. If you have been written up at work, you can look at it two ways: 1) holding a resentful grudge or 2) moving forward with grace and learning what improvements you need to make. Your power lies in how *you* decide to respond. Here are a few thoughts to keep in mind if you are experiencing this situation:

Chip on Your Shoulder

After receiving a complaint, the quickest way to lose your position is to harness a negative attitude and let everyone in the office know that you are upset through passive-aggressive actions. Rolling your eyes, being unresponsive to emails or phone calls, or being condescending will escalate the situation with your employer. What you can control is how you respond.

Blank Slate

If you want to keep your job, drop any attitude you have with your coworkers and move forward to the best of your ability. Asking for additional training or information to avoid mistakes shows you want to continue in the position with a good attitude.

Not Everyone Will Like You

Someone else's opinions of you are not your concern, and there is nothing you can do about it. When people become jealous of another's career or personal life, it is a mirror of what they want themselves. Instead of being jealous, allow that person's success to inspire you. However, if a coworker is upset because they feel you aren't doing your job, it will create resentment. If that's the case, check in with your supervisor to clarify your job description so that you're sure to fulfill your duties and not violate another's responsibilities.

Look for a New Position

If you are discouraged and frustrated because you can't move forward in a difficult work environment, look for employment elsewhere. Life is short, and if you aren't happy where you are, transition into a career that gives you joy.

MINDFUL MOMENT:
If I Had... Then I Would...

If you find yourself working in a job that you dislike, take action to change your life. You are never too old to do something that you always wanted to do. Dreams can come true when you have the inspiration to pursue them! Fill in the blanks and let these questions inspire you to have the life you deserve:

If I had _____, then I would _____.

I always wanted to be a _____.

What steps can you take today to create a change in your life?

_____

_____

_____

_____

Who or what is holding you back from doing what you want to do with "this one precious life?"

_____

_____

_____

_____

Who will support your dream?

_____

_____

_____

Better Customer Relations for Business and Restaurant Owners

In today's global marketplace, consumers can shop and dine any-where, with merchandise and services delivered to their front doors. When delays happen or mistakes occur, the business that agree-ably steps forward to make things right by repairing the business-consumer relationship, is typically the store or restaurant that people will financially support.

Employee Training

Every person who works for you is the face of your company. Training your team on how to interact appropriately with customers, as well as the necessary steps to take when problems arise, is key to your success. From being cheerfully greeted when they enter the store experience, to making a return, every shopper wants to feel like a VIP. Remembering that the "customer is always right" is the smart way to nurture and maintain your business.

With everything that has happened to you, you can either feel sorry for your-self or treat what has happened as a gift. Everything is either an opportunity to grow or an obstacle to keep you from growing. You get to choose.

Wayne Dyer, American author

Customer Complaints

Navigating complaints requires finesse. If a patron is upset enough to make an issue, what happens next is critical. Think about it: They purchased your product or service but are feeling that they did not receive the experience they anticipated. Resolve the issue immediately with a gracious and satisfying solution. You want every customer to feel that their business is especially important to you and in turn, for them to inform others about the exemplary personal care and service you provide. For example, comping a meal in a restaurant or offering a complimentary dessert creates a possible good resolution for the customer.

Point of Contact

Offering a personal connection to follow up on the resolution of a complaint like offering a business card, phone number, or email address as a point of contact in case additional assistance is needed always elevates the customer experience.

Social Media Reviews

Most businesses have a social media presence on crowdsourced review platforms where positive feedback and negative complaints can be posted. Having the awareness of what customers are saying creates an opportunity to provide a meaningful response by thanking them for their compliments or addressing their complaint with an apology followed by positive action they can take to create a quality experience in the future.

Apology Letters to Customers

When it is necessary to respond to a customer complaint with a letter of apology, reference Chapter 2, subheading How to Apologize: The Six Rs. Keep these essential points in mind when writing to your patrons:

Realization: You *know* there was an issue or error.

Remorse: Feeling sorry for the problem to the extent of what's appropriate to the situation.

Reacting: Apologize to the customer as soon as possible for the mistake.

Responsibility: Take action as soon as possible. Handling customer complaints swiftly makes people feel like a priority to your business.

Restitution: Make amends. Do what you can to make things right with your customer.

Resolution: Release. If the customer continues to cause issues, review the actions you have taken or let them take their business elsewhere.

Your customer apology letter need not be lengthy but should read something like this:

> Dear (Name of Customer):
>
> Thank you for letting us know about your (product/meal/service) that you (received/when you dined with us/service on date). Our sincere apologies that your experience in our (store/restaurant/service) did not meet our high standards and fell short of your expectations.
>
> As a token of our gratitude for your business,

please find enclosed a (gift card/discount code) to be used the next time you (shop/dine) with us. Your business is important to us, and we sincerely regret any inconvenience this might have caused you.

Please don't hesitate to contact me personally if you have any further questions, comments, or concerns. Thank you.

Sincerely,
[Business Owner/Manager/Customer Support]
Contact Information

Meaningful Heartfelt Words for Customer Service

Here are sample phrases to inspire you when letting your customers know you care about their business:

Our sincere apologies that your (customer/store experience/ name of product/meal) did not meet your (satisfaction/ expectation).

Please accept this discount code to be used the next time you (shop/dine) with us.

Your business is important to us. Please contact our customer service manager, (name), so we may address your (shopping/ restaurant) experience.

Please accept this gift certificate for a free entrée or dessert.

Please use the code SORRY10 the next time you shop with us to receive a 10 percent discount.

We'd like to reimburse you for the shipping.

We would like to replace the product.

We would like to refund the cost of your meal.

Please find my contact information below.

Please reach out to me the next time you (shop/dine) with us.

We appreciate your patience and understanding. Your feedback is important to us.

We apologize for the delay. Please accept this coupon for a future purchase.

We apologize that your issue was not resolved and that we did not meet your expectations.

We are investigating the situation and will get back to you as soon as we can. In the meantime, we apologize for the error. If you have any questions, please contact (name) at (phone/email).

Oops ... Email Blast Apologies

As an increasing number of businesses embrace digital marketing campaigns, technical glitches are common. When an email blast is sent in error or with incorrect information, a follow-up email to correct the misinformation is important. Apologizing and taking immediate responsibility for the mistake is the best course of action. Including a discount code or free shipping will keep your customers satisfied and help to dissuade them from unsubscribing from your communication.

MINDFUL MOMENT:
Taking Care of You in the Workplace

When juggling our busy schedules, sometimes we become thoroughly absorbed with everything we think we *have* to do instead of what we *need* to do: take care of ourselves first. Awareness that self-care is a priority is another key to our success because feeling good about our physical and mental health keeps us vibrant. Remember to keep these self-care routines in mind every day. You deserve it.

Exercise for Mental Health

Daily exercise is a healthy outlet for mental health and an important part of our self-care. Physical activity allows us to move the heaviness out of our bodies, clear our minds, and alter perspectives. Going for a run, walking on a break, or just taking the stairs, will create a shift, allowing us to step back before reacting in emotion. Work with your healthcare provider to create a plan that works best for you.

You Are What You Eat!

If you are taking care of everyone else except yourself, eventually you will run out of gas. Eating nutrient-dense foods, meal prepping, and packing a healthy lunch are excellent ways to take care of your body.

Take the Time Off

If you have an hour for lunch but typically work through it, step back and think about how much better you would feel by stepping away for the hour and giving yourself the break you deserve. If you are putting off a vacation because you think the company can't function without you, think again. Take the day off; everyone needs a break to replenish.

Setting a Boundary Between Work and Personal Time

Creating a separation between our personal and work lives is very important. Everyone needs time to recover, recharge, and reset. If you are reaching out to your employees over the weekend, give them the respect they deserve by honoring the boundary between work and personal time. Unless it's a crisis, everything can wait until the next business day.

What are some changes you can include in your daily routine to take care of yourself in the workplace?

_____

_____

_____

_____

_____

_____

_____

_____

_____

_____

_____

_____

_____

_____

_____

_____

_____

The best thing to give to your enemy is forgiveness;
to an opponent, tolerance; to a friend, your heart;
to your child, a good example; to a father, deference;
to your mother, conduct that will make her proud of you;
to yourself, respect; to all others, charity.

Benjamin Franklin, United States Founding Father

It's said in Hollywood that you
should always forgive your enemies—because
you never know when you'll have to
work with them.

Lana Turner, American actress

Chapter Ten

ALL THE WORLD'S A STAGE

There is something incredibly magical about being in the brilliant spotlight of fame. Some people strive for it, actively seeking opportunities to propel themselves in front of the public, while other notable figures arrive simply by the circumstance of their achievements. On the other side, notoriety is equally achieved by behaving in a shocking manner that is contrary to the norms of societal standards. Regardless of how you get there, everybody wants a glimpse of you, to be you, or to have a look inside the illusion of your seemingly glamorous world. Being in the limelight is an extraordinary position to be in that carries great responsibility, but when a reckless decision or thoughtless word is taken out of context, it could shatter your career. Carefully crafted apologies are then required in the hopes of repairing a tarnished public image. Major corporations and small businesses also navigate the spectrum of public support—their revenues depend on it. If your company values aren't in alignment with the consumers that buy your products, or your employees are publicly complaining about unfair practices, sales will dwindle and stock value will decline. Whom you endorse is also fair game for public scrutiny. If that person's behavior becomes controversial, a corporation can immediately pull its endorsement deal, resulting in catastrophic financial loss—all because of a mistake.

In today's world, accountability and being in alignment with what is fair and just has become the norm while the public shaming of cancel culture is on the rise. How do you repair your public image after you have been ostracized for an error in judgment? Or worse, wrongfully accused? No matter your stature in life, we are all human so it is our nature to make mistakes—it is how we learn. In this chapter you will learn how to be mindful of the public presence when writing your mea culpa statement and carefully navigating the media storm, no matter who you are.

Mindfulness of Your Public Persona

Thanks to technology, it seems every detail about our lives is searchable online. While some people choose to be reclusive, others use social media as a public microphone to announce the intimate details of their lives or to declare a political battle cry. Being mindful of what you say and do is important to your reputation and what you post reflects your core beliefs. Keep these thoughts in mind when you are on the public stage.

Be Respectful

Maintaining an awareness of respectful and considerate engagement with all people, always and everywhere, is crucial because that is the reputation by which you are known. Being respectful of the laws of the land in which you live or where you visit is equally important. If someone upsets you, step away and refrain from engaging in a verbal or physical altercation, and protect yourself by seeking legal advice.

Be Thoughtful

Our words are powerful tools that can thoughtfully serve to create peace or become weapons that might instigate war. Before speaking your position on a sensitive issue, first consider all sides of the situation and the possible ramifications of offending someone, a culture, or a group of people. Sometimes it is better not to have an opinion if it is outside your expertise.

Be Discreet

A public figure, as well as anyone, can use social media to their advantage and benefit from all its perks and financial rewards. These digital platforms allow us to engage directly with fans and customers as well as to spread awareness. Use them responsibly to empower and bring attention to causes you believe in.

Be Yourself

The only way to live a meaningful life is to always be your authentic self and be open to learning how to be a better human being. If you are asked to maintain a public image that is in alignment with a brand you are paid to endorse, stay true to that, otherwise it is not worth your while.

Be a Light

Use your platform to be a light for others, inspire change, and make a difference in the world. That is how you will truly shine and always be remembered.

The Art of the Public Apology

Being a public figure comes with a tremendous amount of responsibility not only to yourself but also to your family, the people who work for you, the brands you represent, and perhaps your fan base. If you have said, done, or posted something that has created a public reaction, *before* you take any action, step back. A single moment of stress reveals the true character of the person we really are. Before you respond impulsively, get the support you need from the people who care about you, and keep the following information in mind:

Meet with Your Team

The team of people you have chosen so carefully should be your trusted advisors. Whether it's a family member, publicist, or an attorney, consult with them when putting together your strategy for the best course of action to mitigate damage.

Understand the Perspective

It's very important to understand *why* there has been an outcry or reaction from the public's point of view.

Social Media Post

To delete or not to delete, that is the question facing most people when something they have posted leads to controversy. If it's offensive, delete it. Not removing the post reenforces your position. Carefully crafted "apology posts" have become quite common to aid in the repair of thoughtless missteps.

Get Ahead of the Story

Your personal life is your private business. If someone comes forward with negative information to tarnish your image, it's best to come clean and accept responsibility if it's true. Additionally, if someone is threatening you with extortion, consult your attorney and consider your protections under the law. Admitting the fault, apologizing, and taking responsibility puts you ahead of the story and helps to extinguish threats that might not otherwise go away.

Crafting the Mea Culpa Apology Statement

The ability to craft a meaningful apologetic statement that expresses regret, acknowledges the error, and explains how one has learned to be a better human being is an art form. When a public figure is caught in wrongdoing, the evidence is often quickly distributed to the public, making it difficult to deny culpability. In addition to what you learned in Chapter 2 with the Six Rs: Realization, Remorse, Reacting, Responsibility, Restitution, and Resolution, consider these thoughts when writing your mea culpa statement to acknowledge your error:

Communicate

Posting a genuine written apology on your website or social media for the mistake that was made is the best way to immediately express your regret. Always disable the ability for public "comments" under your post thread in your settings.

Understand

Meet with the person or group that felt offended or harmed. Ask what you can do to shed awareness on their cause and follow through with your support. While financial donations are the most common reparation, consider other actions you can take to generate peace.

Learn

Get help for yourself by going on a spiritual journey, getting mental therapy, or some form of rehabilitation. Remember, you are human, just like everyone else. It's our nature to trip and fall from time to time. Learn from your mistakes, then move on.

Heal

Once the remorseful apology and amends have been made, move forward. Create the space for personal healing with forgiveness for yourself. Being out of the spotlight for several months during this recovery time and cocooning in self-care is very healing.

Enlightenment

As a caterpillar transforms into a butterfly, think of emerging after the event as a new, smarter, and more resilient human being. If you choose, doing reflective interviews with the media will allow you to speak about the experience and shed light on what occurred.

Somebody asked me the best piece of advice I ever got. Actually it's so crazy easy, and I say it to a lot of people. But it's really surprising how hard it is, but the sooner you figure out that other people's opinions of you are none of your business and it literally doesn't matter what they think of you—you become free, totally free.

Reese Witherspoon, American actress

Not Apologizing for Who You Are!

Being proud of who you are and what you stand for needs no apology. Just because others do or believe differently from you does not mean you owe anyone an apology for embracing what gives you joy. "Sorry, but I'm not sorry" may sound sarcastic, but empowerment goes with it. Mindfully own what you feel and blaze your trail.

Meaningful Apologetic Words on the Public Stage

When you need the right words to support you in the public eye, here are some apologetic words to inspire you:

I realize what I (posted/said/did) was completely insensitive.

I realize my words were insensitive and inappropriate.

I deeply apologize for my thoughtless and insensitive words that caused harm.

It was never my intention to cause harm; for that I apologize.

I apologize to anyone who I may have offended by my thoughtless (words/actions).

I apologize to (my team/my family/my organization) for my lapse in judgment.

I am so grateful for the opportunity to make myself a better person and shed light on this critical issue.

I ask that you give me the time and space to heal.

I was wrong, and I deeply regret my behavior.

This moment has created a learning opportunity.

I am ashamed . . .

I am embarrassed . . .

There is no excuse for what I did . . .

I take full responsibility for my actions.

I am working on myself . . .

I am getting the help I need . . .

After the Public Apology: Recovery and Redemption

After you've made the sincere apology, as well as the amends that follow, at what point are you forgiven in the court of public opinion? Access to worldwide digital tools enables everyone with the ability to not only post salacious content but also fabricate false information that continues to condemn, even when public figures are innocent or have served their punishment. Do we have the right, once justice has been served, to continually harness hostility by pointing fingers at another when we are not the victim? Do we have the right to sell and create false content for profit? Who are we to judge when every one of us has made a mistake ourselves? Keep these points in mind as you carry on:

> Pray you now,
> forget and forgive.

William Shakespeare, English
playwright, *King Lear*

Maintaining the Company Image

Despite your act of contrition, your endorsement deal or position is dropped because your error violated the company's moral image. Accept their decision and be gracious, because how you choose to react may determine the possibility of future deals.

Taking the High Road

Despite anyone's opinion, if you have meaningfully apologized and repaired the damage, move forward. If people continue to harass you, set personal boundaries. But let your actions speak for themselves. Continue to be kind.

Continue to Do Good Work

Hiding in the shadows and being fearful that everything you do might be criticized will hold you in a personal prison. Hold your head high and live your life with grace. What people think of you is none of your business, and you cannot control their thoughts.

Wrongfully Accused in the Court of Public Opinion

When you have been falsely accused publicly, finding forgiveness is beyond comprehension, especially when the accuser's single purpose is to secure financial gain for themselves by creating the malignment and destruction of your character. A facial expression, the placement of a hand in a photo, or a recorded conversation taken out of context can quickly be twisted from an innocent event into something inappropriate.

Before you scroll through social media believing a scandal story that may or may not be true, or casting judgment, think about how you are actively participating in the destruction of someone's life. Remember, Internet trolls are scavengers who are paid every time you click on their story or watch their salacious videos.

Keep these thoughts in mind if you are being wrongfully scandalized:

* Don't *ever* dim your light because someone is blinded by your personality or success. Be your fabulous self.

* The truth always comes out. You might not believe it while you're in the turmoil, but it will one day.

* Don't hide because you are afraid of being on the front page; stand tall, confidently speaking the truth.

* Continue to do good in this world. The people who love you will show up and stand by you.

The weak can never forgive. Forgiveness is the attribute of the strong.

Mahatma Gandhi, Indian lawyer and activist

The Tree of Peace

Iroquois legend tells of the Great Peacemaker, Deganawida, who, with Hiawatha, brought together warring Native American tribes to form a confederacy to settle their disputes and create the Great Law of Peace. Recognized for centuries as a symbolic gesture of peace, the "bury the hatchet" ceremony was a demonstration to seal their agreement. The chief of each tribe buried a hatchet under the roots of a large white pine tree, where an underground river would magically wash away the weapon. In the 1644 document, *Jesuit Relations*, Reuben Gold Thwaites writes that Native Americans, "Proclaim that they wish to unite all the nations of the Earth and to hurl the hatchet so far into the depths of the Earth that it shall never again be seen in the future." Many tribes also celebrate peace, brought about with forgiveness, by honoring the Great Spirit and the four directions—north, south, east, and west—as well as the ceremony of the sacred "peace pipe."

I wasn't saying whatever they're saying I was saying. I'm sorry I said it, really. I never meant it to be a lousy anti-religious thing. I apologize if that will make you happy. I still don't know quite what I've done. I've tried to tell you what I did do, but if you want me to apologize, if that will make you happy, then okay, I'm sorry.

John Lennon, musician and songwriter

MINDFUL MOMENT:
Global Forgiveness Day, July 7

Every day is a good day to release hurt feelings that do not serve you. On Global Forgiveness Day, being mindful while scanning your heart to clear your consciousness about anything you want to forgive or ask forgiveness for is an excellent action in your healing. If you're celebrating your forgiveness freedom online, mark it with the hashtag: #GlobalForgivenessDay.

I want to forgive (name of person/incident/myself) for:

_____

_____

_____

_____

_____

_____

_____

I ask forgiveness for:

_____

_____

_____

_____

_____

_____

_____

The Fourfold Path of Forgiveness

Nobel laureate, Archbishop Desmond Tutu, and his daughter, Mpho Tutu, cowrote *The Book of Forgiving*, which details the process of walking through the steps of forgiveness and how it is the "greatest gift we can give ourselves." Their work is an essential resource for healing our world and restoring peace following the ravages of war, imprisonment, and racial divide. The concepts and mindful tools of forgiveness they convey apply to everyone. Here you will find summary highlights of the Fourfold Path of Forgiveness from their magnificent work to support you on your spiritual journey to release suffering and create the personal freedom of forgiveness:

1. **Telling the Story:** Sharing the story of what happened allows us to begin the process of forgiveness by releasing it. There are several considerations for achieving this. Tell the story because it gives you the ability to restore your dignity. Tell the truth because the truth keeps us from pretending the harm didn't occur and brings it into the light. Take back the traumatic pieces of what was taken from you and start with the facts. The cost of not telling keeps you bound in victimhood and trauma, keeping you "at the mercy of that tragic experience," while deciding whom to tell and sharing your story with a therapist, friend, or loved one is a good step. Ideally, if you can safely speak to the person who caused you harm, or write a letter you might choose not to send, "There is a profound reclaiming of dignity and strength when you are able to stand in front of your abuser, stand in your truth, and speak of how that person hurt you." Telling the story directly to the perpetrator is a delicate matter when the

perpetrator continues to justify their hurtful behavior, yet it can "increase the likelihood that telling the story will lead to resolution rather than more conflict." Telling the story publicly creates healing and comfort not only for yourself but for others also searching for forgiveness.

2. **Naming the Hurt:** In doing so, "We give voice to our hurts not to be victims or martyrs, but to find freedom from the resentment, anger, shame, or self-loathing that can fester and build inside us when we do not touch our pain and learn to forgive."

3. **Granting Forgiveness:** "We choose forgiveness because it is how we find freedom and keep from remaining trapped in an endless loop of telling our stories and naming our hurts. It is how we move from victim to hero. A victim is in a position of weakness and subject to the whims of others. Heroes are people who determine their own fate and their own future. Many people will carry grudges and resentments for years, believing this will somehow hurt the other person. In truth, it often only hurts the one who carries the grudge or resentment. Many of us live our lives believing that hating the person who hurt us will somehow end the anguish, that destroying others will fix our broken, aching places. It does not. Some seek this path, and it is only when they stand in the aftermath of destruction, amid the rubble of hatred, that they realize the pain is still there. The loss is still there. Forgiving is the only thing that can transform the aching wounds and the searing pain of loss."

4. **Renewing or Releasing the Relationship:** Only you can choose whether to keep someone in your life or after thoughtful consideration, to release the relationship. "We can't create a world

without pain or loss or conflict or hurt feelings, but we can create a world of forgiveness ... that allows us to heal from those losses and pain and repair our relationships. *The Book of Forgiving* shares the path to finding forgiveness, but ultimately no one can tell you to forgive ... we invite you on the journey."

MINDFUL MOMENT: *The Magic of Chocolate*

It isn't a mystery why ancient cultures have embraced the magic of chocolate. From ceremonial rituals to healing the body, or indulging in its flavor, chocolate is used as a remedy for grounding through a difficult time.

The next time you are feeling out of body, try this mindful moment: Take a small piece of chocolate. Gently unwrap it. Hold it in your hands and observe the color. Is it dark, light, or white? How does it feel? Is it melting under the heat of your fingers? Inhale its fragrance. What kind is it? When you are ready, place the chocolate on your tongue. Without chewing, feel its presence there for a moment. Is it melting? What does it taste like? Allow the chocolate to roll around in your mouth for a minute before biting into it. Enjoy the full divine flavor of this delicious moment.

How different was this experience of eating something mindfully and using all your senses? Do you feel better?

_____

_____

_____

_____

_____

How can you incorporate this practice into the foods you eat and the choices you make?

_____

_____

_____

_____

_____

_____

_____

You know, people go on and on about, like,
you have to forgive and forget to move past something.
No, you don't. You don't have to forgive, and you
don't have to forget to move on. You can move on
without any of those things happening. You just
become indifferent, and then you move on.

Taylor Swift, American singer and songwriter

Please watch out for each other and
love and forgive everybody.
It's a good life, enjoy it.

Jim Henson, American puppeteer

Chapter Eleven

MAY THE FORCE BE WITH YOU . . . ALWAYS

The concept of an afterlife has consumed the thoughts of man since the beginning of time. The question is, do our deeds on this Earth follow us into the next realm? What about the concept of good versus evil, or a belief in karma—that what you give, you get?

Many people who have passed and come back to life speak of seeing their life in review and they are transformed by the experience. They speak of seeing a brilliant white light and the overwhelming feeling of love. Some feel the presence of God, angels, their ancestors, and friends.

As we walk through this journey of life, it is part of our imperfect human nature to make mistakes. It is how we choose to make things right again for ourselves and with others that allows our souls to evolve, reaching that higher state of enlightenment in truth and knowledge. It makes sense that spiritual practices honor a Higher Power and embrace the concept of forgiveness so that our conscience may be cleansed not only in this life but into the beyond.

No matter what your spiritual beliefs are, we are all interconnected to one another as humans. That stunning thread of positive light we give to others reflects back, connecting and intertwining us … that light of love between us should never dim.

While some people leave their handprints on our hearts, others may leave memories of misery. How do we find forgiveness with those who have passed on and left us behind, those who we are unable to apologize to for our behavior? In this chapter, you will learn how to create mindful forgiveness with the departed, finding comfort in the spirit of forgiveness.

Finding Forgiveness When Our Time on Earth Is Limited

When we learn that we are facing the end of our life, a wave of unique and unexpected awareness washes over us. Suddenly, we have an epiphany of the importance of life and the realization of looking back at the relationships we want to heal before our last breath. The hurt feelings, hateful grudges, or destructive behavior that separates us becomes meaningless.

We cannot change the past but asking for or giving forgiveness in the final moments of life is a transformational opportunity to peacefully make amends. Rather than rush to someone's bedside, or pray that person comes to yours, clear the air now so you are assured that you did everything possible to heal the heart.

In addition to what you learned in Chapter 2 and Chapter 3, keep these thoughts in mind when you are extending the olive branch:

Call

Make the phone call and speak to the person if you can. Whether or not they accept your apology, you'll know you offered it meaningfully and the gesture was made to create peace. That is all you can do.

Correspondence

If speaking to the person is too difficult, write a letter and express your feelings.

Mediator

When one becomes incapacitated, our loved ones, trusted friends, and spiritual advisors may carry our heartfelt message for us in the hopes of healing any divide.

Taking It to the Grave

When someone spitefully refuses to apologize to you or accept your forgiveness, just remember that no one gets away with causing harm; it will catch up to them. My mother always said, "Leave it in God's hands." That you must do to find peace.

MINDFUL MOMENT: *Reviewing Your Life*

As we go about our busy lives, it feels like time is endless, until something changes. Sudden departures, accidents, or sickness instantaneously bring us to the core of our hearts, creating the possibility of forgiveness. Instead of waiting for catastrophe, consider the following questions:

How would you really feel about a continued separation from someone if you knew you had only thirty days to live?

_____

_____

_____

_____

_____

What would you do with the time you had left?

_____

_____

_____

_____

_____

Who would you make things right with by apologizing?

_____

_____

_____

_____

_____

With whom would you make amends by accepting their forgiveness?

_____

_____

_____

_____

_____

What are you waiting for?

_____

_____

_____

_____

_____

It's not an easy journey to get
to a place where you forgive
people. But it is such a powerful place because it frees you.

Tyler Perry, American actor

Apologizing to and Forgiving Someone in Spirit

It can be distressing to continue to live in anguish over things that were said or done to you by someone even though the person is *no longer living.* Our thoughts and feelings may be just as raw now as when the damage was done. Equally difficult is not being able to apologize for your thoughtless words or actions that caused harm to someone else who has passed on. How can you reach into the beyond to create the peace you so desperately need? In addition to the information you learned in Chapter 2 and Chapter 3, keep these ideas in mind:

Physical Release

As openly and honestly as you can, tell someone you trust what happened to you or what you did. There is freedom in releasing the energy from your body as you convey your truth; it is incredibly healing.

Written Release

If you cannot speak it or share what happened by verbally expressing it to someone else—write a letter, including as much detail as you can with the resulting consequences. Then release the information by burning the letter, shredding it, or burying it . . . whatever works for you. Purging creates energetic cleansing for yourself and is incredibly therapeutic.

MINDFUL MOMENT:
Writing a Letter to the Departed

Write a letter to someone who has passed away before you could apologize to or find forgiveness with them. Allow yourself to write this letter freely and not withhold anything you want to express.

_____

_____

_____

_____

_____

_____

_____

_____

_____

_____

_____

_____

_____

_____

_____

Forgiveness is the final form of love.

Reinhold Niebuhr, American theologian

Spiritual Forgiveness Around the World

Every culture around the world honors the sacredness of forgiveness in some form that is in alignment with their traditions. There is much we can learn from one another and gain different perspectives. Here are a few highlights that may resonate with you:

Greek Mythology

In ancient Greece, the goddess Eleos was the spirit of mercy, compassion, and pity in a time when law and justice prevailed. Her counterpart is the Roman goddess Clementia, whose name means "tolerance."

Judaism: Yom Kippur, "Day of Atonement"

The holiest day of the year for the Jewish faith is Yom Kippur. It is a time of fasting, deep prayer, reading from the Torah, and connecting to God so one many be cleansed and purified.

Christianity

Jesus Christ's spiritual teachings on forgiveness have resonated for thousands of years and are documented in the New Testament of the Holy Bible: "Then Peter came to Jesus and asked, 'Lord, how many times shall I forgive my brother or sister who sins against me? Up to seven times?' Jesus answered, 'I tell you, not seven times, but seventy-seven times'" (Matthew 18:21–22). The first Sunday before Lent is commonly celebrated as Forgiveness Sunday.

Sikhism

According to Sikh religious scripture, Guru Granth Sahib wrote, "Why blame other people? I have to blame my own actions; as I have acted, so are the fruits . . . Forgiveness is fundamentally a moral relation between self and others. Where there is forgiveness, there is God." A peaceful religion, Sikhs believe that when you do something wrong and then realize the error and feel remorseful, you can recover by doing "seva" or good deeds, growing from the experience.

Catholicism: Rite of Confession

One must examine their actions and speak with a priest, who will take them through four basic steps: 1) Regret—you must be sincerely sorry for what you have done wrong; 2) Confess—express what you have done; 3) Resolve—determine to amend your life; and 4) Penance—do the penance the priest gives you, which often includes a prayer such as the Act of Contrition.

Hinduism

One must spiritually attain forgiveness by being in a higher state of mindfulness and understanding that we are an extension of God, who is all-loving. According to the Bhagavad Gita, "If you want to see the brave, look at those who can forgive. If you want to see the heroic, look at those who can love in return for hatred."

Celtic Mythology

Over matters of injustice, Rhiannon, the Divine Queen of the Fairies, is heralded as the Celtic goddess of forgiveness, patience, and strength among other virtues. Often associated with a white horse, she is considered a moon deity who offered compassion and love to those who harmed her.

Spiritually Cutting Energetic Cords

Our life energy is so incredibly powerful that we can feel it rising in our physical body when we think of someone or recall a past traumatic event that has hurt us.

We learned throughout this book that holding on to anger can manifest itself in the body, making us unwell, while mindfully forgiving can create the space for healing. The act of spiritually cutting disruptive energetic cords is an action we can take to sever the ties that bind us to someone else. This is a powerful way to release our connection with a toxic relationship, former lover, or even a work relationship. Bear in mind that we *never wish anyone harm.* Our purpose is to release their invisible link to us. Here is a step-by-step way to cut those cords:

* Sit in a chair and envision the person or the experience you want to "cut cords" with.

* Imagine yourself surrounded by a bubble of brilliant white protective light.

* See the energetic cord between you and the person or experience.

* Pray, call in, or ask for the support of a comfortable enlightened presence to be by your side as you release this energy. Choose whomever you resonate with: God, angels, master teachers, guides, gods, goddesses, or even ancestors—it is up to you.

* Now visualize a pair of golden scissors, and say or think as you sever the cord, "With these scissors, I hereby cut all ties of connection with you, and with love and light release your energetic connection to me."

* When you are finished, surround yourself again with the protective bubble of white light, cocooning yourself. If you feel you need to repeat the process, by all means, do so.

Calling in Angelic Support

While doing thousands of intuitive readings with clients all over the world, spiritual self-help author Tanya Carroll Richardson has listened to many stories of pain and grief as well as acceptance and forgiveness. When our hearts are broken, arriving at forgiveness and even acceptance, can sometimes seem like an unendurable journey. The following is Tanya's divine guidance when calling for angelic assistance:

* When dealing with an overwhelming issue, Tanya recommends calling in angels. Angels are nondenominational and work with people of all faiths, cultures, and backgrounds.

* If forgiving yourself or someone else, or even accepting what happened feels impossible, call on Archangel Raphael, the masterful archangel of healing. What you cannot face on your own, you often *can* face with support, and Archangel Raphael's enormous energy signature and grace can support your spirit during a healing journey of any kind.

* Forgiveness is a softening of the heart, and you never have to do it alone. Simply ask for Archangel Raphael's assistance in your thoughts, prayers, or journal.

* Archangels can work with anyone at any time, so call on Raphael as often as you need.

* Notice if you feel an energy shift around you when you call on this archangel, or if you feel any new emotions moving through you. Also stay alert to synchronicities, or meaningful coincidences and signs, which are divine guidance lovingly brought to you from Archangel Raphael.

Generational Prejudice and Forgiveness

Awareness of injustice, outrageous prejudice, and the senseless eradication and destruction of races because of skin tone, religious beliefs, or culture is brightly shining on past and present matters. How do we forgive and make reparations for the enslavement or cultural stripping of people at any time in our history? It is unconscionable, but it continues to happen every day in our modern world.

Having the grace and wisdom now for the atrocities of the past will not change history, but it will allow us to be present and mindful of the irrevocable damage that has created separation and fear between us. We must remember that we are all human beings on this Earth, with equal rights to live our lives. No man, woman, or child is greater than another, nor does anyone have the right to restrict our ability to live.

If you were raised to believe that your beliefs and cultures are superior, you have an opportunity to learn, discover, and embrace the magic of the world around you. Be responsible for your choices and decisions by being open to seeing the unique soul and spirit in every human being, so that you never perpetuate the bitterness of hatred.

Let this sacred wisdom be a force of change to end and release, thereby honoring those who have suffered. If each one of us could be a light of change in our communities, imagine how much more beautiful our world would be.

Prayers of Forgiveness Around the World

Ho'oponopono, "To Make Right Again"
Please forgive me.
I'm so sorry. I love you.
Thank you.

Buddhist Prayer of Forgiveness
If I have harmed any one in any way,
either knowingly or unknowingly through
my own confusions, I ask their forgiveness.
If anyone has harmed me in any way, either knowingly or
unknowingly through their own confusions, I forgive them.
And if there is a situation I am not yet ready to forgive,
I forgive myself for that. For all the ways that
I harm myself, negate, doubt, belittle myself, judge
or be unkind to myself, through my own
confusions, I forgive myself.

Jewish Prayer for Yom Kippur
To those I may have wronged, I ask forgiveness.
To those I may have helped, I wish I had done more.
To those I neglected to help, I ask for understanding.
To those who helped me, I thank you with all my Heart.

The Lord's Prayer

Our Father, Who art in heaven, hallowed be Thy name.
Thy kingdom come. Thy will be done, on Earth as it is in heaven.
Give us this day our daily bread. And forgive us our debts as we forgive
our debtors. And do not lead us not into temptation but deliver us
from evil. Amen. (Matthew 6:9–13 NASB)

Act of Contrition—Catholic (traditional)

O my God, I am heartily sorry for having offended Thee,
and I detest all my sins because of thy just punishments,
but most of all because they offend Thee, my God, who art
all good and deserving of all my love.
I firmly resolve with the help of Thy grace to sin no more and
to avoid the near occasion of sin. Amen.

MINDFUL MOMENT:
Create Your Own Prayer of Forgiveness

The power of prayer is magical, raising our vibrations to a higher source with gratitude, or simply requesting the mercy of forgiveness from ourselves or another. While some organized religions believe in the structure of a specific prayer, what matters is your expression and your intentions for the highest good of everyone.

Write your own prayer of forgiveness.

_____

_____

_____

_____

_____

_____

_____

_____

_____

It is in pardoning that we are pardoned.

Saint Francis of Assisi, Catholic Saint

Forgiveness says you are given
another chance to make a new beginning.

Archbishop Desmond Tutu, Nobel Laureate

Conclusion

Create a Mindful Forgiveness Self-Care Practice

Embracing the benefits of being mindfully forgiving will support your journey to peace by releasing resentment and the grace to meaningfully take responsibility, apologize, and make amends. Here are some final thoughts to continue to harness love, magic, and protection in your life:

Spiritual Self-Protection

Close your eyes and surround yourself with brilliant white light as if you were in a bubble, removing all negativity. In your mind, see the bright radiance covering you from head to toe, like a shield of armor. This is a wonderful practice to do every day, especially when walking into a difficult situation.

Your Breath Is Life

Please remember, our life is connected to our breath. Be conscious of breathing deeply and releasing negative thoughts. When we fear something, we attract it to ourselves. Breathe and release. What you think, you become.

Spiritual Affirmations

In addition to embracing meditative mantras to live by or prayers that protect you, daily affirmations are also powerful. Create your own, post it on your bathroom mirror, download a daily affirmation calendar app, or use something like this:

> I am protected by the light and love of
> (God/the Universe/Spirit/Source).

> I am thankful for every single moment that created
> the resilient person I am today.

Thank you for taking this journey with me as I embraced forgiveness myself. Writing this book has been a transformative experience that created healing in my heart and spirit, as well as my body. Thank you from the bottom of my heart. I wish you love, light, and the protection of God always. XO

May the force be with you.

George Lucas, American film director, *Star Wars*

Resources for Emotional Support

National Institute of Mental Health: https://988lifeline.org/
Provides support 24 hours a day, 7 days a week
    Live Chat: https://988lifeline.org/
    Suicide Crisis Lifeline: send text to 988
    Veterans Crisis Line: call 800-273-8255, press 1
Crisis Text Hotline: "HELLO" to 741741
    Disaster Distress Helpline: call or text 1-800-985-5990

National Domestic Violence Hotline: https://www.thehotline.org
    Live Chat: https://www.thehotline.org
    Text: "START" to 88788
    Call: 1-800-799-SAFE (7233)

Al-Anon Family Groups: https://al-anon.org
    Worldwide support via in-person meetings, online meetings, and resources.

Alcoholics Anonymous: https://www.aa.org

Worldwide support via in-person meetings, online meetings, and resources.

About the Author

Trauma survivor Kelly Browne evacuated her parents during the SoCalGas Aliso Canyon Blowout over Los Angeles—the worst environmental gas disaster in US history. As her mother spiraled into a fatal cancer diagnosis from the toxic exposure, her daughter was thrown from a horse, suffering catastrophic injury. Browne sought trauma therapy for herself and her family, digging deep to embrace the tools she teaches in this book, forging ahead with tenacity, acceptance, and forgiveness while navigating her way to peace amid the pain.

Browne is a well-known gratitude expert on thank-you notes for adults and children. She is the author of the bestselling series in its category, *101 Ways to Say Thank You: Notes of Gratitude for All Occasions* (Sterling 2008, 2nd edition, 2015); *101 Ways to Say Thank You! Kids & Teens* (Cedar Fort, 2015); and *101 Ways to Say Thank You: Notes of Gratitude for Every Occasion* (Adams Media/S&S, 2022).

Thoughts

Thoughts